SHORT WALKS

Buckinghamshire Pubs

Other areas covered in the Pub Walks series include:

Bedfordshire
Berkshire
Birmingham & Coventry
Bournemouth & Poole
Bristol & Bath
Cambridgeshire
Cheshire
Chilterns
Cotswolds
Cotswold Way
County Durham
North & West Cumbria
South Cumbria
Dartmoor & South Devon
Derbyshire
Essex
Exmoor & North Devon
Gloucestershire
Herefordshire
Hertfordshire
Icknield Way Path
Isle of Wight
Kent
Lancashire
Leicestershire & Rutland

Lincolnshire
North London
Middlesex & West London
Midshires Way
Norfolk
Northamptonshire
Nottinghamshire
Oxfordshire
Shropshire
South Downs
Staffordshire
Suffolk
Surrey Hills
Thames Valley
North Wales
South Wales
Warwickshire
Wayfarer's Walk
Wiltshire
Worcestershire
Wye Valley & Forest of Dean
East Yorkshire
North Yorkshire
South Yorkshire
West Yorkshire

A complete catalogue is available from the publisher at
3 Catherine Road, Newbury, Berkshire.

SHORT WALKS FROM

Buckinghamshire Pubs

Liz Roberts

COUNTRYSIDE BOOKS
NEWBURY, BERKSHIRE

First published 1996
© Liz Roberts 1996

COUNTRYSIDE BOOKS
3 Catherine Road
Newbury, Berkshire

ISBN 1 85306 392 4

Designed by Mon Mohan
Cover illustration by Colin Doggett
Photographs and maps by Bernard Roberts

Produced through MRM Associates Ltd., Reading
Printed by Woolnough Bookbinding Ltd., Irthlingborough

Contents

Publisher's Note

We hope that you obtain considerable enjoyment from this book; great care has been taken in its preparation. However, changes of landlord and actual closures are sadly not uncommon. Likewise, although at the time of publication all routes followed public rights of way or permitted paths, diversion orders can be made and permissions withdrawn.

We cannot of course be held responsible for such diversion orders and any inaccuracies in the text which result from these or any other changes to the routes nor any damage which might result from walkers trespassing on private property. However, we are anxious that all details covering the walks and the pubs are kept up to date and would therefore welcome information from readers which would be relevant to future editions.

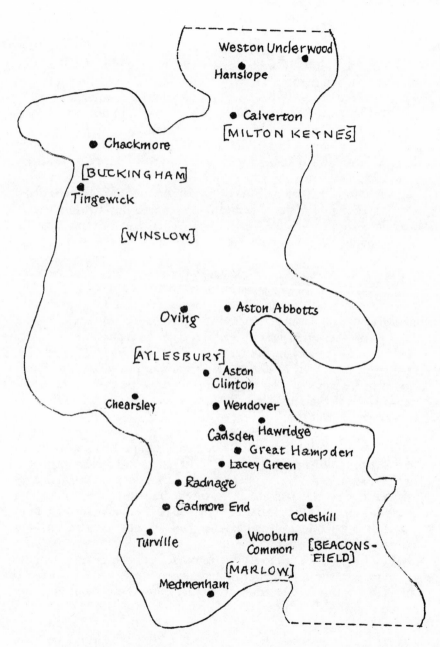

Area map showing the locations of the Pub Walks.

Introduction

Buckinghamshire has always been a county to endear itself to the rambler, the landscape varying from peaceful pastureland and watermeadows to wood-capped hills and deep, dry valleys. It is beautiful at all times of the year. The gentle Chiltern slopes are heavily wooded, mainly with beech, and three small rivers, the Wye, the Chess and the Misbourne, carve their way southward through them to join the Thames, which forms the county's southern boundary. The scarp slopes of the hills drop away dramatically to the rich pastureland of the Vale of Aylesbury and the northern plain beyond, broken by low hills and fed by numerous streams which often lead into the river Great Ouse. Across the hilltops runs the ancient Ridgeway, or Upper Icknield Way, a beautiful and historic route.

All the 20 walks in this book start and finish at a pub where a car may be left while you are out and about on foot – it would, however, be a courtesy to ask the landlord if this is agreeable as, nowadays, a lonely car parked outside opening times can cause anxiety. The description of each inn and its facilities is, as far as possible, accurate, but pubs do change hands, menus do alter and ranges of drinks do vary, so it is as well to check by phone before setting out. Some landlords permit dogs on the premises, some do not, some allow patrons to eat their own sandwiches in the garden, some do not. Just as well to ask first!

The sketch map accompanying each walk is designed to guide walkers from the starting point and give a simple and accurate idea of the route to be taken. The circuits are all along public footpaths or permissive paths but do bear in mind that deviation orders may be made from time to time. For those who like the benefit of detailed maps the relevant OS Pathfinder sheet will be useful. Please remember the Country Code and make sure gates are not left open or any farm animals disturbed.

Many happy hours have gone into the researching and walking of these routes (not to mention the numerous pints of ale downed!) and I hope the reader will gain equal enjoyment from strolling around this lovely county.

Liz Roberts
Summer 1996

1 Weston Underwood
The Cowper's Oak

Pretty, honey-coloured limestone houses and cottages line Weston Underwood's High Street with its unusual cobbled pavements made from a local hard red sandstone. William Cowper, the poet and hymnologist, lodged in the village between 1786 and 1795 in an imposing Queen Anne house, now called Cowper's Lodge. Most of the original manor house, Weston House, was demolished in 1827 but the two impressive gate piers and their adjoining walls, built around 1700, remain. Numerous birds, including peacocks, shriek noisily within the confines of The Wilderness – it is now a small zoological garden.

The Cowper's Oak, dating from 1593, is festooned with a truly magnificent wisteria which blooms flamboyantly throughout the summer. It stands back from the road behind stone steps and would have the appearance of a rather reclusive dwelling house were it not for the inn sign above the door. There is a large, lawned garden with plentiful tables and benches and a good supply of amusements for the young. Hanging baskets adorn the outer walls in season.

Inside is a long, low bar on both sides of the fireplace and, beyond it, a small, quiet dining room where children are welcome to sit if eating. The furnishings are simple – good, solid tables and round-backed sturdy chairs cover the pleasantly carpeted floor. Wide windows overlook the main street and offer a light, airy atmosphere. The walls are hung with a great many photographs and engravings depicting local scenes and people, Cowper and his famous oak tree and an etching of the great man himself, which stands proudly over the piano. Above the mantel is a handsome grandfather clock and there are a good many colourful and decorative plates around the dining room walls.

No less than five real ales are available at any time and, frequently, a guest ale as well. Lagers are also served on draught and house wines, a red and two whites, are sold by the glass. You will also find a very impressive array of single malt whiskies. The extensive bill of fare includes dishes of chicken, fish, gammon steaks and various pies. There are salad dishes, too, and lunches for ploughmen, Frenchmen and fishermen, jacket potatoes with various fillings, vegetarian dishes and a children's menu. Opening times are from 11 am to 3 pm and 5.30 pm to 11 pm on Monday to Saturday, with the usual Sunday restrictions. Food is served from noon to 2 pm and, in the evenings, from 6.30 pm onwards.

Telephone: 01234 711382.

How to get there: Weston Underwood lies between the M1 (reached via junction 14) and the A509 Newport Pagnell to Wellingborough road. To reach the village, either turn off the A509 at Olney or the B526 south of Stoke Goldington.

Parking: There is a good, long car park beside and behind the inn.

Length of the walk: 3½ miles. Map: OS Pathfinder 1001 Olney (inn GR 868508).

This is a peaceful walk between two delightful villages, with magnificent, wide views of typical north Buckinghamshire countryside.

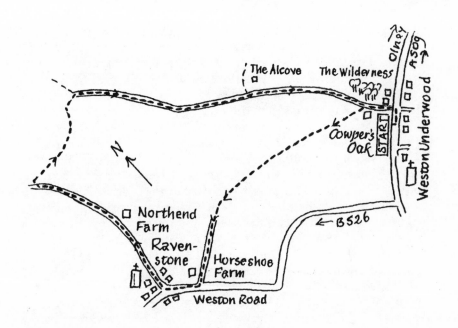

The Walk

Turn left out of the pub and left into Wood Lane. After a very few yards take the path on the left just past a row of cottages and walk diagonally over the field to a gap in the hedge opposite. Cross the stile and a small plank bridge and turn right to walk across the field to a waymarked path in the opposite hedge under the ample shade of a field maple, the only species of maple native to the British Isles. In springtime it is well scattered with small seed 'propellers'.

Go over the next stile here and bear right again to walk alongside a large field, with splendid open views of the lush countryside and the Ouse valley. Cross a plank bridge through a little thicket of woodland and follow the well-marked path over the field ahead, to another stile. Beyond this, follow the path over another field, continuing along the waymarked path. Ahead is Hanslope church, its slender spire the tallest in the county. The squat, square tower of Ravenstone church can be seen downhill on the right.

At a cross-path go over a bridge and through a thickset hedge into the next field, which leads into the outskirts of Ravenstone. Many of the village houses are, or were, owned by the Society of Merchant Venturers of Bristol. Some are still thatched and the thatcher continues to ply his trade locally. On reaching the road,

11

turn right to follow it slightly downhill to the little triangle of grass, on which is the signpost marked 'North End' to the right. The church is approached through a lychgate and is of 11th-century origin. A monument to Heneage Finch is not only in the church but is also to be found in the chequered style of the brickwork of the charming almshouses he built in the late 17th century.

Turn into North End and, just after a view of the church on the left, you will see the double row of almshoues, which originally housed six of the 'indigent poor' on each of its sides. Follow the lane for about ½ mile through beautiful open country scattered with pleasant small houses set back from the road.

At the end of the lane, where it peters out, turn right onto a bridleway and follow this between high, thickset hedges for about another mile or so. From the top of the lane it is possible to see into two other counties – Bedfordshire and Northamptonshire. Hangers Spinney lies on the left, an ancient woodland, mostly of maple and ash. In spring the floor of the wood is carpeted with bluebells and, in late summer, it is possible to hear nightingales nearby. Wild dog roses and trusses of elderflower festoon the hedges and scent the air.

At the junction of the track with Wood Lane turn back just to look at the stone temple known as the Alcove. It was built in 1753 and was a favourite haunt of Cowper. Sadly, the handsome avenue of lime trees which led from the Alcove into Weston Underwood has now been felled. Return to the road and continue along it, past a high stone wall, to the High Street and the Cowper's Oak.

2 Hanslope
The Watts Arms

The small town of Hanslope, nudging the border of Northamptonshire, stands on an arable ridge with splendid views on all sides. Its focal point is the high spire of the church of St James the Great topped by a weathervane in the shape of a whippet with an arrow through one of its paws. The vane was given to the church by a member of the Watts family, squires of the manor, whose life was saved by such a creature during his service in India. The spire, of Ketton stone with four delicately crocheted flying buttresses, is the highest in the county. In the 19th century, Hanslope was the centre of the local lace-making industry, employing, mostly in their homes and schools, around 500 women and children.

The Watts Arms is a tall late 18th-century building, flat-fronted except for two big, blank, brick arches like giant eyebrows on each side of its door. It is white painted with large sash windows looking out onto the road. There is a patio area near the inn with white garden chairs and tables and, beyond it, a grassy play area with swings and slides and plenty of wooden tables and benches. Inside, the walls are adorned with many old prints and photographs of the neighbourhood and surrounding villages. The large lounge bar is carpeted and simply furnished and, off it, there is a games room with dartboard and billiards table. Beyond the bar is a neat and simply furnished dining room with the delightful touch of a small vase of flowers on each table. The inn is said to be haunted by the ghost of one Alexander McKay, a prize fighter and a native of Glasgow who fought illegally with Simon Bryne in nearby Salcey Forest and was knocked unconscious. He was carried to the Watts Arms and laid on the bed in the front room, where he later died. Despite protest by the vicar, his friends erected a stone at his grave in the local churchyard under cover of darkness and inscribed his fate upon it.

This is a Charles Wells house so the cask ales are Eagle and Fargo, alongside a draught Bombardier. On handpump are three lagers, Strongbow cider and Guinness. House wines, one red and three white, are sold by the glass or carafe. There are blackboards in the dining room denoting the extensive menu of good-value daily choices, among them specials for senior citizens, such as fillet of cod, chips and peas. Other delights could be vegetable Mexicana, cheese and onion quiche or a smoked haddock pasta. Beside these, there are a vast assortment of sandwiches, including a seafood triple-decker, home-made soup and roll, crusty and hot, eight different fillings for jacket potatoes, chicken and vegetarian dishes, lots of sweets and a separate menu for children. The staff are young, cheerful and very helpful. Children are not permitted in the bars but can eat in the dining room and play in the garden. Opening times are from noon to 2.30 pm and 6 pm to 11 pm on weekdays and noon to 3 pm and 7 pm to 10.30 pm on Sunday.

Telephone: 01908 510246.

How to get there: Hanslope lies east of the A508 between Old Stratford, north-west of Milton Keynes, and Northampton. Turn off and continue to Castlethorpe, then follow signs for Hanslope, which is some 2 miles further on. The Watts Arms is on the left about ¾ mile into the little town.

Parking: The car park is small but roadside parking is easy and not obstructive.

Market Square, Hanslope

Length of the walk: 2½ miles. Maps: OS Pathfinder 1023 Newport Pagnell and 1024 Milton Keynes (inn GR 803471).

This short, pretty walk with stupendous long views crosses fields where there is little sign of any habitation and then comes upon isolated farmhouses and cottages as it returns, over fields then along Long Street Road, into Hanslope.

The Walk
In order to see the church, cross over in front of the pub and walk up the road opposite between terraces of Victorian cottages, and some of even earlier date, to an attractive little market square, where you take the narrow lane ahead to the churchyard gate. The church is built of light grey limestone and is of 12th to 13th-century origin. It is often kept locked, as is sadly the case with most churches nowadays, but you may be fortunate enough to find someone there and the door open, in which case it is well worth a look inside.

Having viewed the church, retrace your steps to the Watts Arms and enter Gold Street, which quite quickly becomes Long Street

15

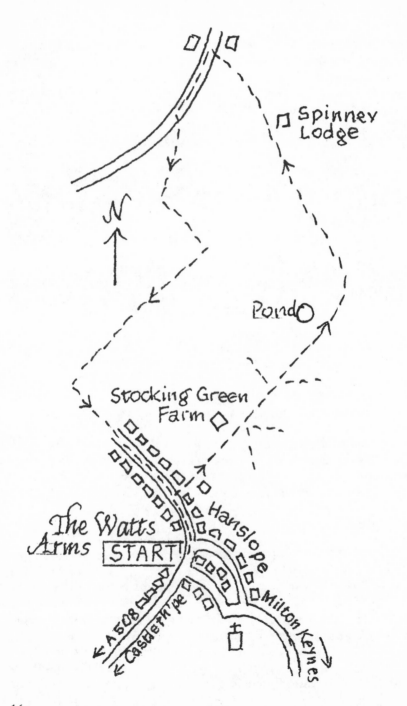

Spinney Lodge

N

Pond

Stocking Green Farm

Hanslope

The Watts Arms

START

A 508

Castlethrpe

Milton Keynes

Road. Walk down it for only about 50 yards to take a marked bridleway on the right, just past Western Drive and alongside Stocking Green Farm buildings. Keep to the bridleway past Stocking Green House and go through a gap in the fence to follow the track toward the traffic now visible on a busy stretch of the M1. Over the field, pass through a gap between two posts, with a hedge on the right, and follow the path ahead. Notice, as you walk, the furrows of ancient strip-lynchet in the grass of the field – a sign of very early cultivation of the area. The views all around are magnificent and the atmosphere peaceful except for the distant drone of the traffic.

Almost at the top of the ridge, bear left to go past a little brake of trees surrounding a small pond on the left and continue over a stile ahead. Cross the next field toward Spinny Lodge and go over a stile tucked quite out of sight in the corner of the opposite hedge. Take the path ahead to another stile in the hedge on the right, then continue over the next field, alongside a ditch or stream and across a small footbridge, to a further stile, carefully concealed in the right-hand corner of the hedge.

This brings you onto a road alongside Yew Tree Cottage, where you turn left for about 100 yards, then take the marked path on the left. Continue on the left-hand path, keeping the hedge on the right, with marvellous wide views, the sky dipping low to the horizon and Hanslope church spire standing out toward the right. Go over two stiles on each side of a ditch and turn right onto a rather tatty path with a tall, straggly hedge on the right. At the end of the field, bear left to cut a corner and cross to a footpath sign in the middle of the opposite hedge.

Now you are back in Long Street Road again, so walk down it for about ½ mile through the more modern part of the little town and turn right at the end of the road to find the Watts Arms just on the right.

3 Calverton
The Shoulder of Mutton

A stone's throw from the river Ouse, which here forms the boundary with Northamptonshire, little Calverton is set in a peaceful, rural area of soft undulations, small fields and quiet lanes. It is quite unbelievable that the edge of the huge, busy conurbation of Milton Keynes can actually be seen from high points in the village. A wiggly lane runs southward to embrace a row of cottages, thatched or brick and tile, belonging to Lower Weald.

The 17th-century Shoulder of Mutton inn is situated high up on a mound on the edge of the village, next door to the lovely rambling, stone, 15th-century Manor Farm. It is approached via its own little drive and stands alongside its modern en suite accommodation, available for longer stays. The inn is of cream-washed stone, low and sturdy-looking, with an abundance of flamboyantly colourful baskets and tubs of flowers to decorate its forecourt in summer. The lawned garden running from the back of the inn has a nice flower border and plenty of practical tables and benches for eating outdoors. Children (and dogs) are not allowed indoors but are made welcome in the garden, where there is also a play area with swings and a variety of toys. Inside is one large, carpeted bar with a pleasant dining area to the left and space for games to the right. There are big fireplaces at both ends of the room, which is simply furnished with dark wood tables and chairs and stools padded with a rich crimson velveteen. The low beams are decorated with brass ornaments.

The guest ale, on draught, is changed every week and there are four other beers, kept on handpump. These are the very agreeable Ruddles County, Courage Directors, Wadworth 6X and Brakspear Bitter. Two lagers are also on handpump as is Scrumpy Jack cider. House wines are sold by the glass and there is a good wine list. The inn is a popular rendezvous for local businessmen from Milton Keynes so it can get quite busy. As for food, daily specials appear on a blackboard by the bar. Everything is home-made, the chips are 'real', the helpings are generous and the prices reasonable. Home-cooked ham and turkey breast are but two of a wide variety of salads, which can also come inside a large chunk of crusty French bread. A favourite special is a ploughman's lunch of turkey and cranberry pie with salad. Vegetarian dishes include a cheese and onion flan. The sandwiches are large and decorated with salad and with a variety of fillings. There is an extensive regular menu of both hot and cold snacks as well as main courses and sweets. The opening times are from 11.45 am to 2.30 pm (3 pm on Saturday) and 6.30 pm to 11 pm, with the usual Sunday hours.

Telephone: 01908 562183.

How to get there: Calverton lies between the A5 and the A422 west of Milton Keynes. Look for a minor road off the Old Stratford roundabout where the A422 joins the A5. Take the first left turning off this minor road, then the first right (signposted Upper Weald) and then turn right at Upper Weald for Calverton.

Parking: There is a large parking space at the rear of the pub, shaded pleasantly by old apple trees.

Length of the walk: 2½ miles. Map: OS Pathfinder 1046 Buckingham (inn GR 789394).

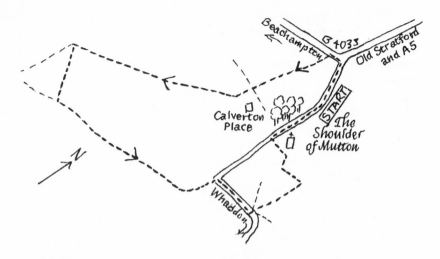

This short, peaceful walk, through some of the most rural of the Buckinghamshire countryside, is undemanding but affords much upon which to feast the eye and rest the senses.

The Walk

Turn right out of the pub exit and walk to the junction with the B4033. Here turn left and walk along the road for 40 yards, over a small bridge, to a footpath signposted on the left. Go over the stile here and walk diagonally right across the field ahead, with the tower of All Saints, Calverton standing out on the left. Pass a little group of hawthorn bushes to reach a footpath sign near a high stone and brick wall. Turn right to walk alongside the wall and go over the stile at the end of the wall through an old apple orchard.

Cross the stile on the far side and walk ahead down the next, long, field, keeping the hedge on the right, with wide views of farmland all around. In this field there is evidence that the footpath follows the route of a minor Roman road leading from Thornborough to Stoke Goldington. It would have passed by Calverton Place, then a small Roman settlement. At the bottom of the field ignore the stile directly ahead and instead turn left to walk along the headland, still keeping the rather untidy hedge on the right. Over the stile in the hedge ahead, turn left onto a track, an ancient way joining Lower Weald to Beachampton, and follow it ahead for about ¼ mile to a metal gate. Go through and continue on the track over an open field toward Rectory Farm.

At the farm entrance turn left to walk a short distance across the bottom of the field to a stile which leads onto a shady little path. Follow the path and turn right after 20 yards or so, over a little bridge and right onto the road. Cross the road to walk on the causeway the short distance, past pretty thatched cottages, to a marked path on the left. Turn left here and go through a dilapidated kissing-gate to follow a path along the side of the field (hedge on the left) to a metal gate, emerging onto a lane opposite the church, the focal point of the village.

All Saints was built over medieval foundations and has a neo-Norman west tower, built around 1810. There is much Victorian stained glass, but particularly to be admired is the rose window at the east end depicting a series of angels on a rich blue background. Opposite the church is a row of rather bleak-looking almshouses and, beyond it, Manor Farm, built in the late 15th century by the de Vere family and extended in the 16th and 17th centuries.

Follow the lane past the farm on the right and the delightful grey stone schoolhouse on the left, to the road again. The lovely trees and lake forming the park-like landscape opposite are part of the Calverton Place estate whose house is not visible from here.

Turn right onto the road to walk along the causeway the ¼ mile or so, past pretty cottages, back to the Shoulder of Mutton.

4 Chackmore
The Queen's Head

The tiny village of Chackmore was home to many of the estate workers when Stowe House was built in the late 17th century. The house, which has been Stowe School since 1923, was by the early 18th century the seat of Sir Richard Temple, later Lord Cobham. Charles Bridgeman, a brilliant landscape designer, was engaged to work on the gardens and, by introducing a ha-ha, he did away with any enclosing fence and threw them open to the countryside. The house was subsequently transformed to be worthy of its surroundings – beautiful colonnades were added to the north front and Robert Adam designed the magnificent south front, both completed in 1770. 'Capability' Brown became Head Gardener in 1741.

The Queen's Head, now well over 200 years old, was the estate pub where local people drank and sang and met to talk over the village happenings – as they do today. Plus ça change! The building sits squarely on the village street, Main Street, its small frontage packed with practical, sturdy benches and tables, its whitewashed exterior decorated with splendid hanging baskets during the summer.

There is an air of warmth and welcome about it. Behind the pub, and entered only through it, is a pleasant garden, enclosed and grassy, with outdoor furniture and children's playthings. Youngsters are not permitted in the bar but there is a very attractive small dining room to the right of it where they are allowed to sit and eat with parents. Both bar and dining room are richly carpeted and plainly furnished with dark wood tables and padded chairs and settles. The windows are deeply recessed and their sills are adorned with china ornaments, while on the walls hang a number of brass plates and a cosy fire burns in the grate on cool days.

A large blackboard alongside the bar announces the day's specials. A superb Irish stew is served with vegetables piled on the plate, the liver and bacon is famous locally and there are always fish and vegetarian dishes. For the less hungry there are omelettes, salads – the home-cooked ham is excellent and generously served – sandwiches and ploughman's lunches with a variety of cheeses or ham. Real ales supplied on draught are Flowers IPA, Worthington and Bass. Also on draught are two lagers, cider and Guinness. Food is served throughout opening hours, which are from noon to 2.30 pm and 6.30 pm to 11 pm on Monday to Friday and from noon to 3 pm and 7 pm to 11 pm at the weekend.

Telephone: 01280 813004.

How to get there: From the A422 between Buckingham and Brackley turn north-west, just ¼ mile from Buckingham, onto an unclassified road signposted 'Chackmore' and 'Stowe'. This goes straight into Stowe Avenue, a mile-long, broad, tree-lined way leading up to the main, now closed, drive to Stowe via the Corinthian Gate. Turn right onto the road signposted 'Chackmore' and immediately on the left is a convenient small, gravelled layby for parking. The Queen's Head is 20 yards ahead on the left.

Parking: The pub has no facility for parking except in the quiet village street. The layby can be used, however, and is seldom filled.

Length of the walk: 5 miles. Map: OS Pathfinder 1046 Buckingham (inn GR 685357).

'Templa Quam Dilecta' – how delightful are the temples – the motto·of the Temple family, is most applicable to Stowe, where the number of temples and ornate buildings far exceeds that of any other English garden. The walk encircles the park and many of these features can be seen. The countryside is typical of the gently undulating farmland of north Buckinghamshire and the walk is not demanding.

The Walk

Turn left out of the Queen's Head and follow the village street for about ¼ mile. Just beyond the houses turn left onto a well-defined footpath, following it to a stile in the opposite hedge. Go over the stile and across the field to a gap in the thick hedge. In spring the scent of the may blossom is heavy as it lies, like thick-fallen snow, on the branches, with brilliant yellow rape fields climbing away on each side.

Go through the gap and over a plank bridge, bearing slightly to the right toward the corner of the hedge on the right. Here follow the hedge round the field ahead, right and then left, to a gap in the opposite side. Go through and, ignoring the left turn, follow the track ahead, bearing a little right and then left, then straight on. High above the trees ahead is the Cobham monument from whose tower it is possible to see into five counties and, to the right, the Bourbon Tower which was once a keeper's cottage but was later renamed to commemorate a visit of the exiled French royal family in 1808.

Walk straight through a gap in a small brake of trees and follow the waymarked path over a wide field, dipping toward the opposite hedge to cross a stream by a plank bridge between two fir trees. Walk leftward across this big field, keeping two houses to the right, to a metal gate alongside a bungalow by woodland in the corner. On the left is the small church where 'Capability' Brown was married, now the only building which remains of Stowe village.

Go through the metal gate and follow the bridleway ahead for 100 yards to the corner of the wood. Turn left to follow a path for 200 yards and then bear left onto a gravelled drive. Follow this ahead and across the Grecian Valley, turning left onto a metalled track ahead. Be careful here not to wander onto the inner, gravelled National Trust path encircling the grounds or you won't get out! The obelisk ahead, erected in 1759, is a monument to General

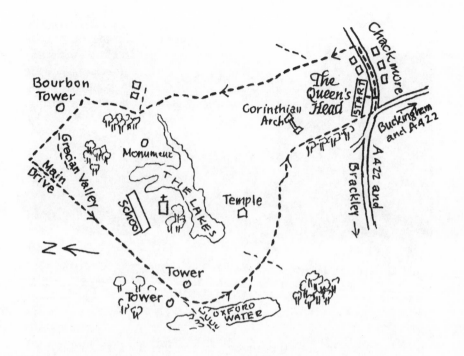

Wolfe. His heroic death during the storming of the Heights of Abraham helped to secure Canada for the British Commonwealth.

At a T-junction, turn left onto the main drive, with the NT car park etc about 100 yards ahead on the left. Follow the drive for about ¾ mile to the two Boycott Towers, situated one on each side of the drive at a crossroads. Below and ahead in the valley are ornamental lakes and the Oxford Bridge, a ridiculous bit of folly with overly ornate urns and rustic stonework, built in 1761. Here take the second path on the left – Queen's Drive – and follow it through metal gates and over cattle grids for 1¼ miles, with beautiful, peaceful, rolling parkland all around. In a dip, there are more lakes and, on the left, a cascade of water tumbling through a rocky cavern from the upper to the lower lake. Also on the left is a rather brashly refurbished temple with a view of the house beyond it through the trees.

The drive emerges before the splendid Corinthian Arch designed by Thomas Pitt in 1765, through which you can look back to see the south face of the house. Turn right here to walk along a charming path beyond the grass verge on the left, under chestnut

The Corinthian Arch, Stowe.

and lime trees, back to the turning on the left for Chackmore and the layby.

Places of interest nearby

The National Trust now owns the landscaped gardens of *Stowe* but not the house or school. The Trust has fashioned a route round the gardens lasting two hours. During the summer, from 4th July to 1st September, the house is open each day from 2 pm to 5 pm. It is advisable to telephone to ascertain dates as the house is sometimes used for private functions (01280 813650). There is a gift shop and morning coffee and tea are served. The Marble Hall of the house and its State Rooms may be visited and the view of the garden from the south portico is one not to be missed.

5 Tingewick
The Royal Oak

Tingewick lies on the busy Buckingham to Bicester road, which the landlord of the Royal Oak likens to a river dividing the village, both sides of which are delightfully rural once away from the main thoroughfare. Upper Street has some fine examples of cottages built of local stone and there is a happy mix of old and new in the High Street.

The Royal Oak lies at the Bicester end of the village, square onto the road, up a few stone steps. Parts of the inn are of 15th-century origin, though it mostly dates from the 17th to the 18th century, and it is not overly 'improved'. The atmosphere is comfortable and airy and an exceptionally warm welcome is encountered in the large, open bar. To the right is a charming dining room with its own small bar, furnished with round tables and beige cloth-covered chairs. To the left is the games room with a billiards table. The inn is said to be haunted by the ghost of a past landlord, who hanged himself in the cellar, but the present incumbent has never been made aware of this sad presence. Children are welcome in the bar and dining room when accompanied by responsible adults. The lawned garden slopes steeply towards the back of the inn and has tables and benches for warmer days.

This is a Banks's house and there are three ales on handpump – Hanson's Bitter, Banks's Bitter and Camerons Strongarm which, as its name would imply, has a real bite to it. Guest beers, such as Marston's Pedigree, are changed each month. Broadlands country wines, elderflower, blackberry and so on, are available and popular and there is a good selection of other wines to be had by the glass. Two lagers, Guinness and a cider are also on handpump. Food available includes sandwiches of beautifully cured and cooked bacon in brown bread with a salad garnish. There are six fillings for jacket potatoes and, proudly presented at the foot of the menu, Black Pudding Thermidor! Barbecues are held in the garden when fine. Opening times are from noon to 3 pm and 5.30 pm to 11 pm and on Sunday the inn is open all day from noon to 10.30 pm. By prior arrangement, the landlord is prepared to extend the daytime hours to cater for parties of walkers or cyclists.

Telephone: 01280 848373.

How to get there: Tingewick is on the A421, about 3 miles west of Buckingham. If approaching on the A413 from Aylesbury, one can turn off north of Padbury and drive to Tingewick via Gawcott.

Parking: There is a large car park on the opposite side of the road.

Length of the walk: 4 miles. Map: OS Pathfinder 1046 Buckingham (inn GR 654328).

The walk visits the pretty village of Water Stratford on the bank of the tiny river Great Ouse and meanders over gently rolling fields, returning over the river at Tingewick Mill.

The Walk

Turn left out of the pub to walk along the High Street to Church Lane, where you turn left again. Just before the church itself, turn left onto a waymarked path, known locally as 'the Gitty', and follow it to the south and west of Tingewick Hall, which was once

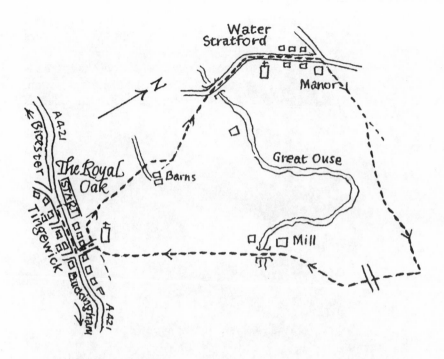

the rectory. Go through a kissing-gate to follow the path over stiles and through fields, keeping the hedge on the right and pausing from time to time to drink in the marvellous wide views all around. Cross a farm track with barns to the right of it to a metal gate and stile and follow the path through the next field, with the thickest hedge now on the left. The hedge is bright with the scarlet berries of hawthorn and viburnum in the autumn. After the next stile bear slightly left to cross the field to a stile in the hedge, 20 yards from the field corner. Bear slightly right now to walk gently downhill toward a brake of trees. Just before the trees is the farm track of Rectory Farm, which emerges here onto the road.

Turn right on reaching the road to walk along it over a delightful little bridge spanning the river Great Ouse whose source is near Brackley, close by in Northamptonshire. It empties into the Wash at King's Lynn. Cattle graze the peaceful watermeadows and, on sunny days, local children paddle in the clear, shallow-flowing stream.

Walk on through the charming little village of Water Stratford.

29

A rather grand gate post, seen on the route.

The road follows the line of a Roman road which ran from Alchester, near Bicester, to Towcester. Here again, there is a lovely mix of old and new buildings – thatched, tiled, brick, stone or timber-framed. The little church of St Giles is raised above the road amid heavy chestnuts and sycamores. It is worth looking at the Norman tympanum over the south doorway, depicting Christ in Majesty within an oval supported by two heavily-feathered angels in flowing gowns. Unfortunately, as is so often the case nowadays, the church has to be kept locked. The Manor House, at the far end of the village, started life in 1598 but has now been divided into several small dwellings and the house itself is much altered.

Just past the Manor House take the footpath on the right over a stile and go across a short field to another one, proceeding across fields and over stiles to a ramshackle brick barn quite high above the village. Here the path runs alongside the barn, so turn right to keep the fence on the right and go on along the well-defined path above and parallel with the river, whose banks are crowded with reeds and overhung with willow. The path leads past a rusty Dutch barn and on down the field straight ahead. Just before the stile hidden in the hedge at the bottom of the field, turn right to cross a small footbridge and a stile. Follow the path, keeping the stream in its deep ditch on the left and moving slightly to the right to find steps up to and down from the embankment of a disused railway, which you cross. At the foot of the steps on the far side is a stile leading onto a path straight across the field ahead. Turn right at the gap in the hedge to walk alongside the next field, keeping the tall hedge on the right.

Bear left across the field to cross the river by a bridge at Tingewick Mill. In the Domesday Book the mill was recorded as being worth four shillings. It ceased working in 1966 and is now a very pleasant dwelling house with a beautiful shady, sloping garden alongside the river. Turn left to follow the lane past the mill for about ¾ mile, over the fields between thick hedges, to the church again and proceed downhill along the lane to reach the main road, where you turn right again to walk back the short distance to the Royal Oak.

6 Oving
The Black Boy

Situated high on a limestone hill amid a huge area of gently rolling clay farmland, the pretty little village of Oving has an enviable position. The church of All Saints and the 16th-century Black Boy are at its western end now that the village has spread toward Whitchurch but they form its natural centre, where the network of small roads and lanes meet. On each side are thatched and half-timbered houses. Oving House, the 'manor', faces away from the village and is an early 17th-century stone house of considerable charm and elegance, with a cupola gracing the roof of its two-storey stables and half-sided parapets added to its north wall in 1743, all commissioned by one Charles Pilsworth, an ambitious young lawyer who later became MP for Aylesbury.

The timber-framed and brick Black Boy sits squarely on the crossroads at the heart of the village. It has an attractive, rambling exterior and enormous grounds. The inn stands at the top of the hill and its garden meanders delightfully downward. A small part of it is cultivated with elegant borders and shrubs but the greater area is well-cared-for mown lawn between trees and shrubs, in all about three acres. It is possible to eat and drink in comfort at a table near the bar or to wander off and sit, still on the premises but quite privately, on the grass among the trees. One can see five counties from this garden. Inside there is one large bar (with fireplaces at each end) approached either through a front door or from a balcony up a few steps from the garden. It is carpeted throughout and furnished with a great many small tables and red leather club chairs. The original beams are decorated with ale jugs and lots of brass ornaments. Beyond the bar is a spacious, pleasantly furnished dining room and, to its right, the snug where a wooden settle holds pride of place. Children are welcome in the snug and the dining room and, of course, in the garden. Though there are no toys as such, it would be a very unimaginative child who could not invent a game in so extensive and idyllic a playing place.

The real ales on draught are Morland Old Speckled Hen and Ansells Bitter. Murphy's stout, Blackthorn cider, Guinness and two lagers are also sold from the pump. House wines are available and these (one red, two white and a rosé) can be bought by the bottle or glass. Bar food is listed on boards to the side of and above the bar and the menu offers a wide choice, ranging from a variety of open sandwiches and delicious crusty bread ploughman's lunches, through steaks (a speciality of the house), duckling, honey-glazed lamb, chicken and fish dishes to vegetarian lasagne. There is a well-chosen menu of home-made sweets. The inn is closed all day on Tuesday but on other days opening times are from noon to 2.30 pm and 6 pm to 11 pm. Food is cooked and served every day except Tuesday both at lunchtime and in the evening. The usual Sunday opening hours apply.

Telephone: 01296 641258.

How to get there: Turn off the A413 Aylesbury to Buckingham road at the northern end of Whitchurch, into a lane signposted 'Oving' and 'North Marston'. Take the second turning on the right to lead you straight into Oving village beside the church and opposite the Black Boy.

Parking: There is a fairly spacious car park alongside the inn and it is also possible to park in the road.

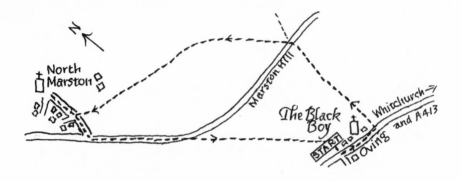

Length of the walk: 2½ miles. Map: OS Pathfinder 1070 Winslow and Stratton Audley (inn GR 784214).

This short walk takes you over the fields to the little village of North Marston, once much visited for its healing waters, with its lovely church. The slopes are quite steep but they are over very quickly and the views are well worth the effort.

The Walk

Turn left out of the pub and walk up Church Lane for about 100 yards to a marked footpath on the left at Church Farm. The right-hand side of the lane is defined by a beautiful cream-coloured stone wall, ivy-clad in some places, behind which stands the imposing red-brick, 17th-century rectory. Turn onto the path, where there is a stile on the right to carry you up a bank away from the very muddy cattleyard. At the far end of the bank go over another stile and then follow the path to go through a big green metal gate on the left. Walk ahead down the field, keeping the thickset hedge on the right, the path meandering gently up and downhill with magnificent wide views all around and the squat tower of North Marston church below and to the left.

Go through a gate in the right-hand corner of the hedge and follow a little path down into Marston Hill road. Cross the road with care as there are blind bends both ways, to two signposted paths opposite. Take the **left** path toward North Marston and walk straight across the field to the stile opposite. Here negotiate the two stiles and walk straight ahead to a gate/gap in the right-hand corner of the opposite hedge. Go through this and walk up the

34

next field, keeping the hedge close on the right. Go through the gate in the opposite corner of the field and proceed uphill past the buildings and house of Burnaby Farm to a stile tucked into the very corner at the top of the field. Walk down the lane ahead to emerge at a T-junction.

Here, on the left, is the village pump and also the Schorne Well or Holywell. Its waters were noted for their healing properties, in particular for eye conditions, and its finding engendered a long period of intensive pilgrimage to the site, with subsequent financial benefit to the good people of North Marston! The well was discovered by a parson, John Schorne, incumbent of St Mary's from 1290 to 1314 and a much-revered local figure. To visit the church, which is very beautiful, one must turn right here and then right again to walk the 100 yards or so to the church gate. The squat belltower is of 15th-century origin while the porch and nave date from the 13th to the 14th century. The side of the church is decorated with a number of crude and grotesque carvings. The raised clerestory, which gives the church its ethereal atmosphere, was built with the aid of the pilgrims' money. The south aisle is the probable site of John Schorne's shrine but his bones were removed

There are extensive views from the pub's garden.

to Windsor – out of pique because the shrine had become so famous. There is a lovely, richly carved piscina in the side chapel.

Having viewed the church, retrace your steps to the pump and well and carry on down the rather ordinary village street. The old village of North Marston was virtually destroyed by fire in 1705, so most of the building is modern and not very interesting. At the end of the street, a small metalled path leads to the main road, Portway. Here, turn left and walk down the road for about ½ mile where, right beside the road sign 'North Marston', on the right, take the left path up the hill, making for Oving, high up ahead, its church tower just to the left. Follow the path diagonally across the field to a gap/gate over a stream under the opposite hedge. Walk ahead, keeping the group of trees to the left. Go over two stiles on each side of a small concrete bridge, well hidden in the opposite hedge, and follow the path uphill, keeping the thick, high hedge near the left. At the top of the field, in the left-hand corner, is another stile, which leads onto a short footpath emerging in the car park of the Black Boy.

Places of interest nearby
Six miles west of Aylesbury, on the A41, is *Waddesdon Manor*. Built in the 1870s for the Austrian branch of the Rothschild banking family, this French Renaissance-style château is now administered by the National Trust. There are important collections of English and Dutch paintings and French porcelain. For further information, telephone 01296 651211 or 651282.

7 **Aston Abbotts**
The Royal Oak

The village of Aston Abbotts, a jumble of houses and cottages, some old and thatched and hidden, some bold and red brick and assertive, is set round two tiny green triangles, shaded by pleasant trees and close to the church of St James, which was restored a mite too heavily by G.E. Street in 1865. However, the lovely Early English south doorway still exists and there is a piscina in the chancel. Attractive lanes wind their way through and round the village, which still has two pubs and a shop.

The Royal Oak, a 15th-century, Grade II listed building with a ghost from some almost forgotten Cromwellian skirmish, fought near Aylesbury, stands sideways-on to the road and has a large car park and grassy area in front of it. Records show that it used to be a butcher's shop and was licensed as recently as 1854. It is a long, low building with a deep thatched roof, timber-framed with curved braces of whitewashed brick and plaster. In summer it is decorated with colourful hanging baskets and a trough of bright flowers will be found by the door. On the left of the house is a large pump and the original fire certificate is still affixed to the wall. Inside, through the flagged and low-ceilinged porch, there is a huge bar, split into three. Intricate patterns of beams and joists are decorated with a myriad of brass implements and ornaments and even a hunting horn. In the centre a huge chimney place has grates on both sides and fires roar in both on cold days. To the left is the games room and bar where children are welcomed, and from here a wide door opens onto a lawned garden with plain wooden furniture, some outdoor playthings and an aviary. On sunny weekends, barbecues are arranged here. To the right is the bar used for the serious business of eating and drinking and, in the far corner down two steps, is the minute snug which is over the top of the original cellar. Opposite the bar is the small dining room where a roaring trade is carried on, especially in the evenings. There is a comfortable atmosphere and the service is prompt, cheerful and friendly.We were told that walkers are always welcome and (with prior notice) often come to tea!

The real ales are Ind Coope, Burton, Bass, Tetley and ABC Best Bitter. Murphy's stout and Guinness are also on draught, and a couple of lagers. Red and white house wines are sold by the glass and Australian red wines are very popular to accompany the chef's steak dishes. Blackboards at the back of the restaurant display the day's specials, most of which are home-made. As well as steaks, in various sizes and guises, there are meat and vegetarian lasagnes, steak and kidney pie, fish and filled jacket potatoes. The many different sandwiches, plain and toasted, are dressed with salad, as are the ploughman's lunches. The opening hours are from noon to 3 pm and 6 pm to 11 pm, with the usual Sunday restrictions, and food is served from 12 noon to 2 pm and 7.30 pm to 9.30 pm.

Telephone: 01296 681262.

How to get there: Aston Abbotts lies west of the A418 Aylesbury to Leighton Buzzard road. Take the signposted turning about 4 miles from Aylesbury and follow the lane for about a mile. The Royal Oak stands on a corner so look out for the inn sign – and the car park comes first!

Parking: The inn has a very spacious but quite unshaded car park, so take the dog out of the car on hot days.

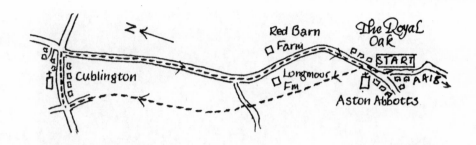

Length of the walk: 3¼ miles. Map: OS Pathfinder 1071 Leighton Buzzard and Stewkley (inn GR 849200).

This is an undemanding and peaceful walk across the meadows between two small Buckinghamshire villages, returning by way of a quiet country lane beside comfortable farmhouses.

The Walk
Turn right out of the pub and walk along the village street past pleasant houses and cottages, ancient and modern, bearing right past the Bull and Butcher public house. Keep walking ahead past the two little triangular village greens under their trees, following the road as for Cublington past St James' church (which also offers Sunday cream teas, in the summer, to walkers and cyclists!) and on past the entrance to the Old Masters restaurant on the left. About 100 yards after this take a marked footpath up the bank on the left and follow it across the restaurant garden to a rather overgrown-looking path in the corner with a stile. Walk straight across the next field to a wide gap in the hedge and go through it to continue over the next field, keeping the hedge/fence close to the left and a view of Longmoor Farm to the right. Here there are lovely wide views of Vale countryside all around and, on sunny days in summer, skylarks can often be heard. From the stile in the opposite fence it is possible, by turning round, to see the lion carved out of the chalk hillside above Whipsnade Zoo.

On reaching a farm track, go over the stile, turn right and, after 20 yards or so, turn left to take a waymarked path over two stiles and straight across the field ahead to another stile. Continue across another field to yet another stile in the right corner. This leads onto

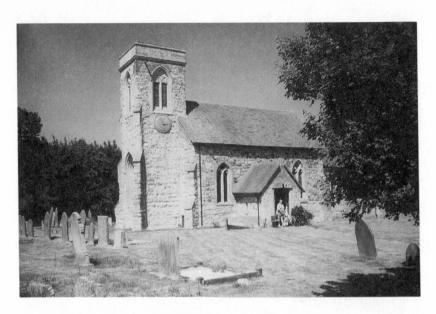

Cublington church.

a metalled farm track where you turn right and very shortly left over a stile to cross another field and go round a dirty pond among trees on the left. Follow the well-defined path across stiles and fields and over a cross-track into a field where it leads beside a tall hedge on the left, with great trusses of dog-rose and elderflower rampaging in season. Turn left and right over a little bridge to follow the path into Cublington, across a field and through trees to emerge onto the road. In the village is a little spinney planted to commemorate the victory of local people over the Government's plans to build London's third airport here.

Turn right to follow the village road past the triangular green and the squat church of St Nicholas, perched on its chalky ridge overlooking splendid Aylesbury Vale scenery toward Whitchurch. At the crossroads take the right turn and follow this quiet lane for 1½ miles back into Aston Abbotts, passing lush farmland and glimpses of wider views through gaps in the hedge. Wildlife such as deer, rabbits and foxes abound around these quiet lanes. The village is entered after passing Red Barn Farm and Longmoor Farm when the restaurant and the church tower reappear. Follow the little street carefully back to the Royal Oak.

8 Aston Clinton
The Rising Sun

The great expansion of the straggly little hamlet of Aston Clinton occurred when Sir Anthony Rothschild purchased Aston Clinton Park (now named Green Park) in 1851 and extended the old house, which no longer exists. Reddish-brown Victorian brick terraces sprang up to accommodate the estate workers and the Misses Rothschild, Connie being then 16, had a village school built for the girls at which they were wont to teach.

The A41 Aylesbury to Watford road runs through the village and the Rising Sun stands on the main roundabout at the centre. It is a plain, square, brick and tiled, early 19th-century house and makes few compromises to present-day fads and fashions. On the Aylesbury side is a long, wide, well-maintained car park with the far corner under the shade of a large tree. Behind the inn is a huge conservatory which is now the restaurant, quietly and tastefully furnished with the facility to draw tables together to cater for parties. At the near end of the conservatory is a glassed-in servery and the far end opens out onto a lawned garden with a pleasantly colourful flower border and a delightful trellis up which a honeysuckle climbs vigorously. The long lawn has ample wooden tables and benches and some children's play equipment. Youngsters are welcome in the garden and restaurant but not in the bars. The inn is entered by a porch and there are bars on both sides, the one on the right being designed more for games and that on the left for the serious matter of eating and drinking. The floors are carpeted and the rooms are furnished with plain wooden tables and padded seats in a muted cretonne. The wallpaper is very typically Victorian and items of Victoriana and old sepia photographs abound.

There are three real ales – Courage Best, Directors and Webster's Green Label. Lagers and Guinness are also sold on draught. The inn features 'wine days' when special offers are made but there is always a comprehensive wine list, with, for example, a much-recommended Australian Chardonnay and a Kentish Lamberhurst dry white. Blackboards around the conservatory entrance proclaim the day's food and wine offerings. The menu is extensive and reasonably priced. Torpedoes are huge crusty rolls with a variety of fillings, including steak, and there are single and double-decker sandwiches. Jacket potatoes come with, among other things, chilli and bolognaise. Main courses comprise unusual chicken and fish dishes, vegetarian meals and, of course, steak and kidney pie. The inn is always busy, though not too busy for a chat and a smile. Opening hours are from 11 am to 11 pm on Monday to Saturday and from noon to 3 pm and 7 pm to 11 pm on Sunday. Food is served all day every day, except on Sunday evenings. Telephone: 01296 630399.

How to get there: The Rising Sun lies on a roundabout on the A41 some 4 miles on the Tring side of Aylesbury.

Parking: There is ample car parking by the inn. For the shorter walk, you drive from the inn to the 'Home Sitters' premises at Buckland Wharf and you can park off the lane, where the stile leads onto the canal towpath.

Length of the walk: 4½ miles, or 3 miles if you drive from the inn to Buckland Wharf and start the walk there. Map: OS Pathfinder 1094 Aylesbury and Tring (inn GR 887118).

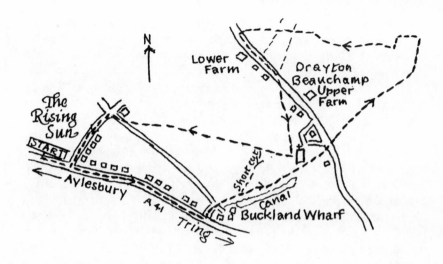

There are no hills on this pleasant walk, which takes you along a peaceful stretch of disused canal and within sight of Wilstone reservoir. You will have superb opportunities to view water birds and wildlife at close quarters on this route.

The Walk
Turn left out of the pub and cross the intersection on the roundabout. Follow the A41 on a grassy, wide path straight ahead for ¾ mile to a turning on the left at Buckland Wharf, on the far side of which stands a tall, square building, once a pub and now the premises of the business 'Home Sitters'. Turn left and go left again and then right over a stile onto the canal towpath, a part of the Wendover Arm of the Grand Union Canal. Follow the pleasant path and, after about 400 yards, the level of water diminishes to the extent that the bed is now dry. Efforts are to be made to restore the water for some recreational purposes but at present it is just a ditch. The countryside is richly lush and peaceful, the only sound that of birdsong. As the water peters out, the trees begin to close overhead to form a cool, green tunnel.

A little further on go through a small bridge and, on the far side, turn left to mount the high bank and then go right to walk above the empty canal for about ¾ mile. To the left are tantalising views of the Wilstone reservoir with Ivinghoe Beacon soaring above it,

43

its tufty clump of trees on top. Woodbine and dog-rose ramble about the hedge and, further left, the huge pile of Mentmore Towers, once the home of Lord Roseberry, floats like a mirage above its tree-capped hill.

The track becomes rough and very uneven for about ¼ mile, going past a tiny path down steps hidden in the hedge on the right and, 20 yards or so further along, there is a path on the left beside a post where there is a marvellous view of the whole expanse of the reservoir. Turn left to follow the clear path down steps and over a stile and then along the field edge, with a tiny stream weaving along beside it. Turn to right and left to follow the field corner. Ahead is the dark mass of the Chiltern escarpment, heavily wooded. At a field corner, opposite a group of farm buildings ahead, take the stile on the right to follow the path across the field on a well-defined track. Go down steps and across a little bridge into a grass field, where you turn left to walk through it slightly diagonally to a group of tall trees in the hedge opposite – a delightful ramble through a lovely scented field of tall meadow grasses and wild flowers and plants in summer. Climb the stile under the trees and stride out across the field to another stile, almost in the left-hand corner of the opposite hedge. Go across the next little field to a stile onto a lane. Turn left to walk past a warm red-brick farmhouse on the left.

After about 100 yards there is a right turn, Church Lane, which you take to walk through the fields towards Drayton Beauchamp church standing quietly back beside the impressive Old Rectory. Enter the field in front of which the church stands by a stile.

If you have left your car at Buckland Wharf, walk diagonally across the field to a stile in the hedge in the left-hand corner. Go over the stile and up a little secret path, then down some steps to emerge again onto the canal bank. Turn right to follow the path the 400 yards back to the bridge and your car.

For the longer walk, go straight across the field, keeping the hedge on the right, to a stile in the opposite hedge. Follow the path over two more stiles and straight across two more fields, to emerge onto a narrow lane beside a row of Victorian cottages. Turn left into the lane and then, at the crossroads, turn left again to walk the ½ mile back to the Rising Sun, which stands on the right-hand corner of the road.

9 Chearsley
The Bell

From the small village green at its centre, the several tiny lanes which make up Chearsley run downhill toward the lush watermeadows bordering the river Thame. In the 1980s, Chearsley was one of the first villages in Buckinghamshire to embark on the production of a parish map, which encouraged the enthusiastic involvement of the whole community. From it came new parish enterprises, one of which was the writing-up of the series of small footpaths running across the village, joining lane to lane, church to school, pub to shop and so on. There is some new building but much of the village housing is still made up of half-timbered and thatched dwellings, the lanes bordered by witchert walls, their tops now tiles rather than thatch.

The Bell Inn is a 16th-century thatched house, also of witchert, a type of clay built onto a stone base and native to this part of the county. It is constructed on a wooden 'cruck' or frame, a horseshoe-shaped beam onto which the clay would have been moulded, and is, interestingly, on the site on which the very first

45

bell for the church was cast. It has a pleasant, whitewashed exterior, which is decorated in summer with masses of colourful hanging baskets. Tables and chairs are set out on the forecourt. Beyond the car park, at the side of the inn, is a large L-shaped garden and patio surrounded by borders of bright flowers and well supplied with practical tables and benches. Food is barbecued out here on sunny Sunday lunchtimes. In one corner are some climbing toys for children, who are welcome both in the garden and the bar provided they are well-behaved, as are dogs. Inside, the flagged and low-ceilinged bar stretches the whole length of the house with a fireplace at each end, one a huge inglenook of old brick which gives out enormous warmth on cold days. A great variety of plates decorate the walls and beams, and on one side a little glass-fronted cupboard houses what remains of the dinner/tea service which was a wedding present to the landlord's great-grandmother.

This is a Fuller's house and the draught beers are the brewery's excellent London Pride and Chiswick, with one other, varying seasonally. There are also three lagers on draught. House wines, a red and two white, are sold by the glass and, for so small a house, there is an impressive selection of French, Australian and Bulgarian wines. The food is imaginative, plentiful and reasonably priced. Especially to be recommended are the brochettes of prawns, asparagus and baby sweetcorn with salad. Sandwiches – doorsteps – are prepared to order and there are three blackboards offering the day's menu, as well as the specials listed above the bar. Meals are not served on Sunday evenings or Mondays, but from Tuesday to Saturday food is available from noon to 2.30 pm and in the evening up to half an hour before closing time. The pub is open from 12 noon to 2.30 pm (closed at lunchtime on Monday) and 6 pm to 11 pm, with the usual Sunday hours.

Telephone: 01844 208077.

How to get there: Turn off the A418 Aylesbury to Oxford road south-west of Stone, following signs to Cuddington. Continue on the narrow road west through Cuddington village, downhill then uphill to Chearsley. The Bell lies on the left of the green at the top of the village.

Parking: Beside the inn or in the lane outside.

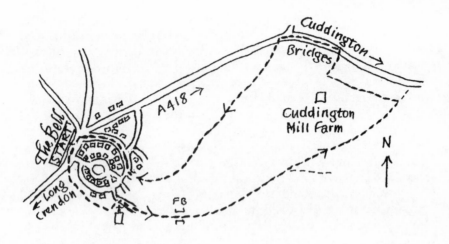

Length of the walk: 3 miles. Map: OS Pathfinder 1093 Ambrosden and Waddesdon (inn GR 718107).

The walk follows the convoluted lanes of Chearsley, past its interesting little church and to a small bridge over the Thame. It continues over wide fields and near the river before returning along more paths and lanes.

The Walk

Turn left out of the pub and follow the narrow Church Lane downhill, past pleasant thatched cottages and modern houses set in pretty gardens high on the grassy banks on each side of the lane. The church of St Nicholas, with its squat belltower, is on the right ½ mile down the lane and is open and well worth a look round, going through the carefully tended churchyard. The early (12th-century) structure of herringbone stonework was part of the original endowment of the then-new Augustinian abbey at Notley, in the parish of Long Crendon. Changes and alterations have been made in later centuries, not least the recent bringing of electricity to the mainly candlelit nave. The font is of Norman origin. There is a large hatchment painted on the north wall but little now remains of the once extensive wall-paintings which decorated both nave and chancel. The welcome lack of heavy Victorian stained glass gives the little church a light and airy look.

Having viewed the church, walk straight on down the lane to the

47

footpath for Cuddington which leads, through a wooden gate, across a meadow to a little bridge over the river Thame. Cross the bridge and bear slightly left toward a row of pollarded willows, walking alongside them parallel with the lazily flowing river, which is adorned with fat, yellow water lilies in summer. Make for a stile in the fence about 30 yards from the river bank. Cross the stile and take the path, bearing right to a gap in the hedge. Go through the gap and walk, as straight as possible, uphill to a stile in the left-hand corner of the opposite hedge. Cross the stile and walk up the field, keeping a fence and then a hedge on the left, to a stile on the left behind a pleasant house and garden about 30 yards from the road. Go over the stile and walk diagonally down the field toward Cuddington Mill Farm, going through the metal gate at the bottom of the field into the drives of Cuddington Mill and Cuddington Mill Farm.

Here turn right to walk the few yards to the road, where you turn left to walk up it for about 500 yards to the second footpath sign on the left-hand side of the road (Thame Valley Walk). Go over a stile to follow the path diagonally across a large field, up and gently downhill to a stile almost in the left-hand corner of the opposite hedge. Go over the stile and across a little wooden bridge and walk alongside the field, keeping the fence on the left. Cross another stile at the field end and go over a small field to another one, then slightly right across the next field to a further one, which leads you onto Lower Green Lane.

Follow the lane ahead past more pretty thatched and timbered houses into School Lane, which emerges onto the main road. Here turn left to find the Bell and its car park.

10 Wendover
The End of the World

The End of the World, thus named because of its proximity to the huge garden centre, World's End, and the lane opposite, lies about a mile on the Aylesbury side of Wendover. The town itself still preserves the air of earlier centuries, mainly the 17th and 18th, in its architecture, though the amusing clocktower on the corner of the Tring road is, in fact, a 19th-century folly and is now a thriving information centre, having previously served to house fire-fighting apparatus and, later, street-cleaning tools.

The inn, dated 1620, lies back from the A413 Aylesbury road on the left, just past two mini-roundabouts. Colourful tubs and hanging baskets decorate the forecourt and, behind it, there is a pleasant lawned garden with white furniture and some children's games. Inside, after dipping your head to avoid the beam, you will find a welcoming, low-ceilinged bar with a plain, flagged floor and wooden tables and chairs. To the left is a small dining room, pleasantly and restrainedly decorated, and, beyond the bar, a light and airy space with more tables and chairs. There are quaint and interesting decorations – figures, fascinating clocks of all shapes and sizes above the deep old fireplace and some impressive examples of agricultural implements. Suspended from a beam is a charming hot air balloon in miniature, complete with basket and its complement of passengers.

The real ales are Greene King IPA and Abbot, with an occasional guest. All are on draught, as are Guinness and three lagers, Harp, Stella Artois and Kronenbourg. An enormous rack of wines stands to the right of the bar, giving a wide choice and house wines, both red and white, may be purchased by the glass. Meals are very substantial and represent good value. Starters include home-made soup and barbecued pork ribs and there are main dishes of fish and meat – particularly good are the herb and garlic breast of chicken and a lasagne. Blackboards about the place denote the day's specials and there are mouthwatering 'afters', such as treacle sponge, spotted dick and fudge cake. Lighter snacks include toasted sandwiches, a great hunk of deliciously crusty French bread with a variety of fillings and jacket potatoes. Children have their own menu and they are welcome in the restaurant and dining room, but not immediately in front of the bar. Dogs, on leads, are allowed in the garden. Meals are served daily between 12 noon and 2.30 pm and from 7 pm to 10 pm on Wednesday, Thursday, Friday and Saturday evenings. Opening times are from 12 noon to 11 pm each day, although the landlord sometimes closes up between 2.30 pm and 5.30 pm if the inn isn't busy.

Telephone: 01296 622299.

How to get there: The End of the World lies on a mini-roundabout at the junction of the B4009 with the A413 Wendover to Aylesbury road.

Parking: There is an ample car park alongside the inn.

Length of the walk: 3 miles. Map: OS Pathfinder 1118 Chesham and Wendover (inn GR 859093).

This gentle stroll leads past the Weston Turville reservoir, with wildlife abounding, and then along the little Wendover Arm of the Grand Union Canal, where, in spring, anxious mother ducks and moorhens fuss over their young.

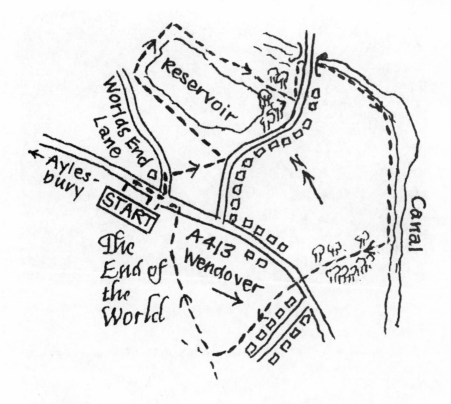

The Walk

Cross the main road (the A413) with care and turn left into World's End Lane, then walk along the pavement for about 25 yards to go right onto a marked path across a large field. Ahead are magnificent views of the steep Chiltern escarpment, towards Tring and Ivinghoe. On the far side of the field, cross a plank bridge and climb the steps to turn left onto the footpath surrounding Weston Turville reservoir. Water birds of many species, including the rare crested grebe, inhabit this peaceful stretch of water and, alongside the path, there is a hide, where birds can be watched while you remain unobserved. Opposite is the small yacht club and in summer craft can be seen coming and going from it.

At the end of the narrow path turn right to cross the head of the reservoir, where the whole expanse of water is revealed. Forget-me-nots, cow parsley, buttercups and dandelions brighten the steep grassy banks while, to the left, there is a splendid view of the tower

51

A bridge over the Wendover Arm of the canal.

of Weston Turville church among trees, with a farm and fields in the foreground. Turn right to follow the path through a narrow woodland area, where bluebells create a marvellously colourful ground cover in springtime.

The path emerges onto a cross-path and here you turn right to walk to a road approached through a wooded gate. Turn left and take the path, just inside the woodland and parallel with the road, leading to the canal towpath, which is part of the Wendover Arm of the Grand Union Canal and is managed as a nature reserve. Turn right onto the path and walk under the small road bridge. A pair of kingfishers nests under the bridge and the birds are often to be seen, perched, totally still, on an overhanging branch, intent on the water. They fly off in a flash of brilliant blue at one's approach.

Follow the towpath for a good ½ mile, passing the wide turning basin for the use of the barges, now a haunt of herons and their young, and continuing beyond a small group of wooden seats set back from the bank. You will eventually reach a half-circle of wooden seats set well back from the path and called 'Rail Crossing'. In fact it was here that the little single-track railway from Wendover to Halton used to cross the canal on its way up to the RAF camp.

Turn right here onto a scruffy little path between high hedges and fields and follow it right through to the A413 again. Cross the road once more to a marked footpath opposite to walk for ¼ mile between allotments and the backs of colourful gardens to a steep little dip and a stream, then a cross-path. Turn right onto this path and climb over the stile just ahead.

Walk straight on across the field, keeping a straggly hedge, a duckpond and the re-emergent stream on the right. This field is often full of sheep so it is advisable to keep dogs on the lead. Across in the far left-hand corner of the facing fence is another stile. Go over it and turn right and then left, following the path along the field edge to a gate in the hedge after about 130 yards. Turn right through the kissing-gate and follow the grassy path to a wooden gate leading onto the verge of the main (A413) road. Turn left and the inn is a little further along, across the intersection.

11 Hawridge
The Rose and Crown

The tiny hamlet of Hawridge, a cluster of red-brick houses, the large white edifice of Hawridge Court, a small church and the inn, lies along one of the half-dozen 'fingers' which reach uphill from the 'palm of the hand' which is Chesham town. Close by lies Cholesbury Common. Views from the ridge on either side are splendid, particularly spectacular when autumn colours the leaves of the trees or spring brings out the carpet of bluebells, the tiny oxalis and the pure white windflowers under the pale green canopy of the beeches.

The Rose and Crown lies smack on the road, in front of a lawned garden with sturdy wooden tables and benches. Do sit outside if the day permits as the view is superb down the valley and through the trees, many of which flower in the springtime. It is also permitted to eat your own snack in the garden provided you buy a drink to go with it. Dogs on leads are also allowed out here. Inside is a large, comfortably furnished bar with a real log fire burning in the winter. There are plenty of chairs and tables, flowers in the bay windows and softly played classical music to accompany the warm welcome from the landlord. Children may join you in the small dining area.

There are seven varieties of real ale from which to choose. All are on draught, as are the excellent ciders, Red Rock and Strongbow. House wines, both red and white, sweet or dry, are available by the glass. The food is generous and appetising and includes such favourites as chicken provençale, steak and kidney pie and delicious home-cooked ham. Cheesecakes, chocolate fudge cake and treacle tart may tempt the unwary later. Food is served from noon to 3 pm (2.30 pm on Sunday) and from 6.30 pm to 9 pm every evening except Sunday, when the chef has a rest. Opening hours are from noon to 3 pm and 6 pm to 11 pm (10.30 pm on Sunday).

Telephone: 01494 758386.

How to get there: Turn northwards off the A416 Berkhamsted road from Chesham just on the edge of the town, signposted 'Hawridge' and 'Cholesbury'. The Rose and Crown lies on the right about 3 miles along this quiet, scenic road.

Parking: There is a good-sized car park behind the inn.

Length of the walk: 2½ miles. Map: OS Pathfinder 1118 Chesham and Wendover (inn GR 948062).

This gentle route through spectacular scenery is undemanding and absolutely right for a stroll after lunch at any time of the year.

The Walk

Turn right out of the pub and walk a few yards along the road, then turn left into a flinty little lane just past a public telephone, Hawridge Lane. The track is waymarked and as it leads between tall, overhanging hedges it can be muddy after rain. There are staggering views of the rolling farmland through gaps in the hedge and in the spring, needless to say, bluebells and primroses are clustered around the roots of the trees. The lane leads gently downhill into a valley where, on the right, there is a wonderful pattern made against the grass by a plantation of young fir trees, marching in line.

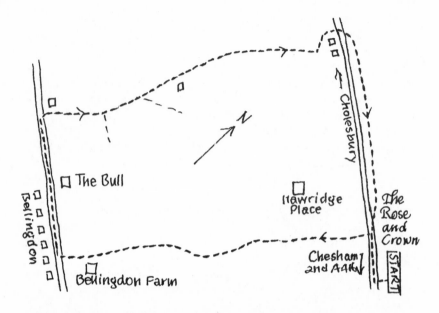

The path then leads gently uphill past Bellingdon Farm and emerges onto another 'finger' at Bellingdon village. Turn right onto the road, continuing past some very comfortable-looking houses set back in pleasant gardens on the left and, presently, the Bull public house on the right.

About 100 yards past the pub turn right off the road onto a waymarked track, a drive with wide grass verges leading to two dwellings. Walk on past the first of these and then, where the path divides, take the left-hand path over (or under) a broken-down stile and across the field ahead, past a small cottage on the right to a double stile in the opposite hedge.

Go over these stiles and follow the path straight ahead through the extensive plantation of young firs, dark and light green with the occasional pink of the emergent pine cones – a huge field of Christmas trees in the growing. Go over the stile in the opposite hedge and follow the path steeply uphill over a grassy field, through a gap and, ignoring a cross-path near Hawridge Place, sitting grandly on the right, emerge onto the road again through a wooden gate in the left-hand corner of the next field by a small red-brick house.

Cross the road to the opposite verge and turn right to follow the grassy path across the exit of a small lane onto the road and back to the Rose and Crown on the left.

Places of interest nearby

Just north of Berkhamsted town centre, on the other side of the A41, is *Berkhamsted Castle*. This ancient fortification, Norman in origin, can be viewed all the year round and is open from 10 am to 4 pm. Telephone 01604 730320. At Tring, to the north-west, is the *Walter Rothschild Zoological Museum* with over 4,000 animal species on show from fleas to whales and butterflies to sharks. The collection is a branch of the National History Museum and the perfectly preserved specimens are housed in a unique Victorian setting. Due west of Hawridge but south-west of Wendover is *Coombe Hill*, the highest point in the Chilterns at 258 metres. The views from here are tremendous with the Vale of Aylesbury to the north-west, the Cotswolds north of Oxford to the west and the Berkshire Downs to the south. You may also see glimpses of Chequers in woodland to the south-west — it is of course the official country seat of the prime minister. However, it is the people of Wendover we have to thank for all these views, as it was they who established the public rights of way over Coombe Hill in 1906 when the private owner of the land fenced off the hill and denied the public access. The hill is now in the care of the National Trust, (although the monument on the top is still private property) as is the adjoining beech woodland, Low Scrubs — parking for both these properties is available just off the Dunsmore road.

12 Cadsden
The Plough

This delightful little pub has the advantage of being both on the Ridgeway and on its own small lane off the main Risborough to Great Hampden road, huddled below a high bank of trees on the one side and a hugely steep scarp slope of the Chilterns toward Whiteleaf Cross behind it. Its exterior is simple and square but it has sat there for over 200 years. Plain red brick and a slate roof give it the appearance of an ordinary dwelling; only its cheerful inn sign, and the rapidity with which the car park fills at the weekends, proclaim its purpose.

Inside there is a bustling and cheerful atmosphere of friendly welcome in the low-ceilinged and beamed bar, which extends the length of the building and can have a roaring log fire going at both ends on a cold day. The furnishing is simple – large plain wooden tables are surrounded by chairs and padded banquettes. Various brass ornaments adorn the walls and beams. There is no garden as such, but a plentiful supply of wooden benches and tables are available on the grassy area on the other side of the lane, where shade or sunshine can be chosen on warm days. Children are permitted in the bar if they are eating and it is tacitly understood that the left side of the bar is for non-smokers.

Four ales are served on draught, among them the very popular Theakston Bitter. Lager and Guinness are also on draught and wines may be bought by the glass. There is also a wine list. On two large blackboards to the left of the bar are listed the specials of the day. The pub is famed locally for its pies, especially the beef and ale, but other dishes, such as minted lamb casserole, vegetable lasagne and fish dishes, are available too. For a lighter snack, much to be recommended are the bacon and cheese skins – baked potato skins, emptied of their original contents and filled, instead, with a mixture of cheese and bacon. There are various salad dishes and the Ridgeway Ploughman's, which is huge. Hot home-made soup often appears: Opening hours are from 11 am to 2 pm and from 5 pm to 11 pm, except on Sundays when the times are noon to 2 pm and 7 pm to 10.30 pm.

Telephone: 01844 343302.

How to get there: Turn eastwards off the A4010 Princes Risborough to Aylesbury road at a roundabout, which, if you are approaching from the south, is approximately 1 mile from the decontrol sign at Monks Risborough. Follow the lane, signposted 'Cadsden' and 'Great Hampden', and continue for about 1 mile before turning right on an almost blind bend on which stand two or three cottages and the inn.

Parking: In front of the pub or in the large car park among the trees.

Length of the walk: 3½ miles. Map: OS Pathfinder 1118 Chesham and Wendover (inn GR 825045).

There is some dramatic scenery on this short walk through glorious woodland, but the uphill bits are all quite manageable.

The Walk

Turn right out of the pub and go over the stile in the left-hand corner under a beech tree beyond the garden, following the track ahead parallel with the car park. This is a charming avenue of young poplars, carpeted with bluebells and violets in early spring, and later

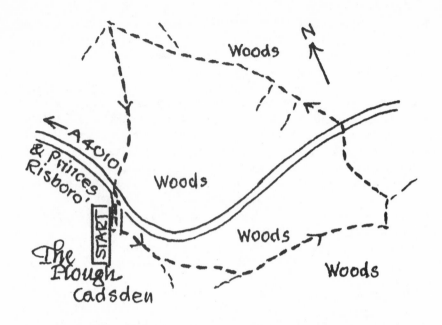

on the bold blue clumps of borage are set off by the paler blue of forget-me-nots. The woodlands loom high on either side.

At a junction of several paths, by a huge clump of borage, choose the third from the left, not the one with an arrow on a tree nor the beckoningly broad one along the valley floor, but the middle one. Follow this well-used track gently uphill, ignoring side turnings and bearing left, still on the main track, where the scene on the left drops dramatically into a deep, dry valley. The cool green of the young beech leaves in the spring is beautiful and the bluebells are riotous. Follow the track until a big metal gate is reached. Go through the wooden gate alongside it and continue ahead for about 20 yards to where, at a cross-path, you turn left onto a broad track leading gently downhill. The presence of dog's mercury and white-flowering woodruff indicate that the woodland is quite ancient, as these plants take a long, long time to establish.

Shortly, a sign indicating a bridleway will appear on the right. Bear right as if to mount a stile ahead on the indicated footpath but instead turn left and follow the bridletrack downhill, ignoring all side turnings and bearing left into open country at the valley foot, having ignored the waymarked path on the right. The next part of the walk, a rather boggy track bordered by trees on the left and open fields with grazing horses on the right, is nearly always muddy so come prepared. Escape routes have been cut in the worst of the places.

The bridleway emerges onto a lane which you cross to a wide open space, often used as a car park, then turn left to follow a broad track for about ½ mile, ignoring the side turnings. The very steep hillside looms tall on the right and the path clings to a ledge, with the woodland falling away alongside into the same dry valley. These heavily wooded valleys often occur on the scarp slopes of the chalky Chilterns, having been scoured out at the end of the Ice Age when the ice thawed and water rushed down to be gulped into the chalk before it could reach the clay soil to form rivers like the Thames.

The path continues gently downhill between towering grey trunks of beech trees and, here and there, the huge up-ended flat plates of tree-root systems, a convoluted jungle forming a wonderful habitat for insects and small mammals. Soon the view opens up spectacularly on the left with a magnificent panorama of the whole Vale of Aylesbury spread out in lush greens and blues below and,

Woodland views on the walk from Cadsden.

on the horizon, the giant cooling towers of Didcot power station some 12 to 15 miles away.

At a broad cross-track, signposted 'Ridgeway' to the right and ahead, turn left downhill to go through a handsome gate and straight ahead. The immediate foreground is filled with a mixture of scrubby trees and bushes and the rounded, more colourful heads of trees ahead while, beyond them, the smooth green of Whiteleaf golf course is topped by another, darker, headland of hugely tall beech trees.

Where the path diverges into three, take the extreme left option and follow it through a wooden gate ahead, a little way up and then a little way down to the main road again. Turn left to cross this with care on the bend and bear to the right into the lane leading to the Plough and its car park.

Places of interest nearby
South of Princes Risborough but 1½ miles north of High Wycombe is *Hughenden Manor*. This was the home from 1847 until his death in 1881 of Benjamin Disraeli, the legendary Conservative politician. The house still contains his furniture and many of his personal effects and is said to be haunted by his ghost. There is access to some fine woods on the manor's parkland estate and the house and garden are open at 1 pm to 5 pm, on Wednesday to Sunday from May to October. The park is open all the year and further information is available on 01494 532580.

13 Great Hampden
The Hampden Arms

High on the Chiltern escarpment and surrounded by beech woods and rolling farmland, the hamlet of Great Hampden has an enviable position. This is superb walking country – the hills offer magnificent scenic views into the deep valley below, the broad fields are edged with thick hedges, bright with wild dog-rose and elderflower, while deer, rabbits and pheasants are often to be seen hurrying about their business. From the bewildering number of paths criss-crossing this glorious area, I have chosen one short walk. This will, I hope, whet your appetite for more of this lovely countryside which has a special sort of beauty at every season.

The Hampden Arms stands on the corner of a road junction, four-square onto the road with, on its left, a long, lawned garden and, on its right, a small car park. Hanging baskets adorn its front in summertime. Much of the inn is of 17th-century origin but there have been later additions to the building, probably early 20th century. The bar, down a step and leading off the charmingly furnished snug/dining room, has a wealth of old beams, now ornamented with horse brasses. The whole room is cheerfully carpeted and simply furnished with square tables of light and dark wood and chairs, covered banquettes and settles to match. Children are not permitted in the bar but are welcome in the snug and, of course, in the garden, where there are plenty of tables and benches, with or without shade, and sun umbrellas. The variety of trees is interesting – sycamore and thorn and the odd wild cherry among them.

There is a good choice for the drinker here. Ales on draught include Wadworth 6X, Thomas Hardy (quite a strong and unusually bitter flavour but nice), Tetley and Abbot Ale. Addlestone's draught cider is also available, as are two lagers and Guinness. House wines, a dry, a medium white and a very drinkable red, are offered by the glass and there is a huge wine list. If you are looking for a quick nosh-up, forget it! You won't find it here, in this award-winning inn. The chef specialises in fish dishes and produces a delicious medley of shellfish in a bed of salad or there is a plaice fillet grilled and served with an appetisingly 'different' sauce. You will also find home-made chicken and brandy pâté and the Hampden Nudger, a huge sausage smothered in onion gravy. There are numerous vegetarian dishes, very popular among these being a stir-fry of assorted vegetables accompanied by a delicious sauce. The helpings are very generous, the choice enormous, everything is attractively presented – and the four blackboards around the bar walls give some idea of the excellence and variety of the cuisine. Served only at lunchtime and advertised on the bar, lunch-brunches offer beef cannelloni, jacket potatoes with a range of fillings and club sandwiches, which include a three-decker of chicken, ham and salad, for a quicker meal. The inn is extremely popular so it is advisable to phone in advance if you are in a party; bookings are not made for the garden so you take pot luck there. Opening times are from noon to 3 pm and 7 pm to 11 pm (10.30 pm on Sunday). Food is served from noon to 2 pm and 7 pm to 9.30 pm.

Telephone: 01494 488255.

How to get there: From Great Missenden take the unclassified road for Princes Risborough and, after about 3 miles, choose the second turning on the left for Great Hampden. Turn right at the crossroads at the top of the hill and follow the lane as it winds its way to the pub about a mile further along on the left.

Parking: There is a gravelled car park alongside the pub and, behind it, a field which is used as an overflow.

Length of the walk: 2 miles. Map: OS Pathfinder 1118 Chesham and Wendover (inn GR 845016).

There are no hills and few stiles on this delightful walk and, as well as beautiful scenery, there is a charming church, John Hampden's manor house and pretty cottages and gardens to see.

The Walk
Turn left out of the pub and cross the road to go up a small lane on the right alongside some cottages. After only a few yards, take the waymarked path through a gate on the right. Follow the path ahead, first beside some cottage gardens then alongside mixed woodland and out into open countryside, with splendid wide views all round and the odd pheasant to trip over in the autumn. Cross a farm track and go through a gate opposite towards Great Hampden church, across the fields and past a little brake of lovely sweet chestnut and beech trees surrounding a pond. If you are lucky enough to find a 'holy duster' or a flower lady at work and the flint and stone-faced church open, it is well worth a visit.

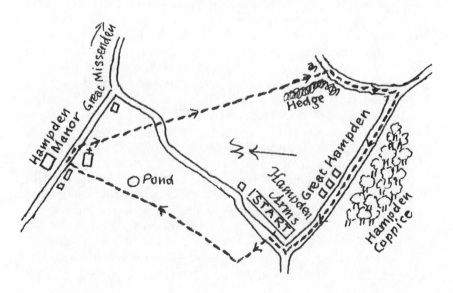

Great Hampden House.

Inside is a monument to John Hampden, who died in 1643 of wounds sustained at the battle of Chalgrove Field. This was designed for his grandson in 1743 and is of two cherubs, one of whom appears to be waving a funny hat, seated on a sarcophagus surmounted by a large oval medallion depicting the battle. Walk to the left of the church and onto the drive of Hampden Manor, the home of John Hampden and, indeed, of successive Hampdens from the 11th century until recently. The house embodies parts from the 14th to the 18th century but today, with its low battlements and muddy rendering, it looks the Gothic revival building that it largely is. King John's tower, on the south front, may well be 14th century while the hall behind has a genuine medieval roof. John Hampden, cousin of Oliver Cromwell, is most famous for his refusal to pay the notorious Ship tax imposed by Charles I. It is said that he rode his horse from his home, down into the valley and across the hills to Great Kimble church, where, during Morning Prayer, he disrupted the service to rally his tenants to follow his example.

Turn right onto the drive and follow it to a small pedestrian gate, just past the churchyard on the right. Go through the gate and across the field, bearing slightly right, to another small gate in the opposite hedge, emerging onto the road. Cross the road to a stile opposite and follow the path ahead, for the first part between an avenue of tall trees to a stile in the right-hand corner of the hedge, and then, keeping the tall hedge on the right, follow the path to the end of the hedge and straight on across the field, making for a gap in the opposite hedge. The views are huge, edged darkly with beechwoods and, in summer, skylarks sing above the cornfields.

Go through the gap in the hedge and turn right onto a tiny lane, which you follow, ignoring a path sign on the right 50 yards ahead, to a T-junction at a small triangle of grass. Here turn right again to follow the lane past pretty houses and cottages and, soon on the left, the dense woodland of Hampden Coppice. At another junction walk straight ahead onto a more major road, signposted 'Great Hampden', and soon Hampden Common appears on the left. The last Hampden (Earl of Buckingham) to live in the house was a much-loved and respected 'Squire', known to all the villagers. A great cricket enthusiast, in 1950 he organised the laying of the cricket ground on the common and the pavilion opposite. The ground is surrounded by woodland, edged purple in late summer by great trusses of rosebay willow herb. The cricket ground and the road to it were dedicated by the villagers to the local people who fell during the Second World War. At the corner of the road stands the Hampden Arms.

14 Lacey Green
The Pink and Lily

Lacey Green village is strung out on a narrow chalk ridge which descends finally into Hughenden Valley. Its most remarkable feature is its 17th-century smock mill. Originally built in Chesham, it was brought to this location in 1821 where, it is presumed, it functioned for some years. It must have fallen into desrepair before being taken over by the Chiltern Society and restored in 1972. Its position, high on the ridge, makes it a local landmark.

The Pink and Lily was a haunt of the poet Rupert Brooke and his friends before the First World War and some of his poetry is proudly preserved here. Though the pub has been modernised, with the addition of a glass conservatory/dining room, the original taproom remains much as it always was and has plain wall benches on a red-tiled floor, a deep inglenook with a low mantelpiece and facilities for dominoes, cribbage and shove ha'penny. There is unobtrusive piped music. The airy main bar is furnished with comfortable pink plush seats and an open fire burns merrily on cold winter days. The dining room is approached through wide arches and has white garden tables and chairs, while the long, grassed garden contains plenty of wooden tables and benches for outside eating and drinking.

Numerous real ales also are available, well-kept on handpump – Boddingtons, Brakspear, Flowers Original, Doctor Thirsty's Draught and Hobgoblin, Ind Coope Burton, Wadworth 6X and Wethered. The food is home-made and efficiently served by the friendly staff. Beside sandwiches and ploughman's lunches with various additions, there are jacket potatoes with a good variety of fillings, a roast of the day, steak and chicken dishes, all with fresh vegetables, and various vegetarian options. Delicious, reasonably priced, home-made desserts are also on offer. Wine may be purchased by the glass and there is a comprehensive wine list. Meals and snacks are served at lunchtimes and in the evenings every day except Sunday evenings. Opening hours are from 11.45 am to 3 pm (11 am on Saturday) and from 6 pm to 11 pm. On Sunday the times are from noon to 3 pm and 7 pm to 10.30 pm. Children may join adults in the dining room and there is a special menu.

Telephone: 01494 488308.

How to get there: Lacey Green lies to the east of the A4010 between Princes Risborough and High Wycombe. South of Princes Risborough, turn off at a crossroads signposted for Lacey Green and Speen. After a wide right-hand bend, follow the narrow road steeply uphill to turn left for Parslow's Hillock. The Pink and Lily lies 1 mile down the road on the right.

Parking: Ample, in the car park alongside the pub.

Length of the walk: 3 miles. Map: OS Pathfinder 1118 Chesham and Wendover (inn GR 826019).

This pleasant but undemanding walk leads sharply downhill through mixed woodland and follows the sloping lane back to Lacey Green.

The Walk
Turn right out of the pub and almost immediately right again into Lily Bottom Lane, walking along it for about ½ mile to Lily Bank

69

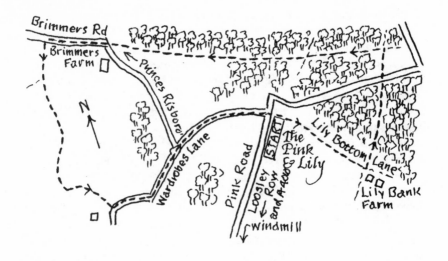

Farm, lying on the right. You take the gravel track on the left just before the farm buildings – the footpath sign is obscured in the thickset hedge. After a few yards, fork left onto a waymarked bridleway through pretty mixed woodland, leading onto a road. Cross the road to the lane opposite and walk along it for about 150 yards to reach a waymarked footpath on the left into woodland.

Follow the well-defined path straight ahead, ignoring all cross-tracks and diversions. In spring the woodland is carpeted with bluebells and, between the clumps, the curled-up tips of young fern emerge from the dead-leafy ground. After crossing a wide bridleway, the path begins to descend quite steeply into a deep, dry valley. Views through the trees of the surrounding rolling farmland and wooded hills are stupendous. The path finally descends very steeply by way of steps and emerges into open country over a stile. Walk down the fields ahead, keeping the hedge on the right, and go out onto Brimmers Road on a sharp bend. Don't turn left but keep straight ahead along the road, preferably, for safety's sake, on the wide grass verge, past Brimmers Farm and on for approximately 200 yards to a waymarked bridleway on the left between two brick posts.

Follow the bridleway past the entrance to Hill House and bear right alongside the house, where the track narrows through thickly overhanging hedges, in summer bordered by clumps of yellow archangel, with the pungent scent of cow parsley filling the air.

Carry on along the track and through a gate, then past a very pretty house to emerge onto Wardrobes Lane.

Turn left to follow the lane quite steeply uphill through beechwoods, and at the T-junction at the top, cross carefully to the Pink and Lily opposite.

Places of interest nearby

From Lacey Green (and from the Great Hampden and Cadsden walks) you are within easy reach of the *Home of Rest for Horses*, a worthwhile charitable trust situated at Westcroft Stables, Speen Farm, Slad Lane, near Lacey Green. Here they look after over 120 horses, ponies and donkeys, and are open to the public from 2 pm to 4 pm daily and throughout the year. Telephone 01494 488464. Further afield is the *Chiltern Open Air Museum* at Newland Park, Gorelands Lane, Chalfont St Giles. Here you can experience a working farmyard from the Victorian era, explore a medieval field system and discover what it was like inside a 1940s prefab. There are special events, including craft fairs throughout the year, and the museum is open from 2 pm to 6 pm, on Tuesday to Sunday from April to October. There is recorded information on 01494 872163.

15 Radnage
The Three Horseshoes Inn

Radnage is a large parish made up of many 'Ends' – Bennett End, Church End and Town End, to name but three. All are divided from one another by rolling Chiltern hills and deep, dry valleys, sometimes open and sometimes wooded. Lovely dense beechwoods crown most of the hills and stride along their ridges, while the valleys are intensely farmed with fields of corn surrounded by ancient hedgerows and bisected by a multitude of footpaths and bridleways. The rambler's paradise indeed!

The Three Horseshoes lies, not surprisingly, just up a tiny thoroughfare called Horseshoe Lane and dates from 1745. It is an attractive, low building of red brick and tile, with a great many small windows on all sides – the better to admire the stupendous views it affords of the local countryside. Behind it is a small but perfect garden overlooking a deep valley and the hills beyond it. The front of the pub is adorned in summertime with copious hanging baskets, window boxes and tubs to give a splendidly colourful effect. Inside are two bars. To the left is the Country Bar, retaining its genuine atmosphere of age and comfort, with an uneven flagged floor, a huge old coal or wood-burning stove and a real old-fashioned bread oven alongside it and charming cushioned settles around the walls. To the right is the Lounge Bar, again low-ceilinged and beamed but carpeted and elegantly furnished with small tables and padded stools and sofas to sit on. The licensee and his family make charming hosts and welcome one with warmth. Children are allowed in the bar, as are dogs, provided both are well-behaved.

The real ales served are Flowers Original and Brakspear ordinary, both well-kept and flavoursome. Cider, Guinness and a lager are also on handpump. Wines are sold by the glass and there is a comprehensive but carefully selected wine list. The menu for the day appears on a board on the wall by the bar. All food is delicious, reasonably priced and home-cooked. Several traditional pub meals, such as gammon steak, chicken, steak pie and fish and vegetarian dishes, are served, beside sandwiches and ploughman's lunches of pâté, Stilton or Cheddar cheese. The evening menu is a little more extensive. No food is served on Sunday evenings and the inn is closed all day on a Monday. Opening times are from 12 noon to 3 pm and 7 pm to 11 pm on Tuesday to Saturday, with the usual Sunday hours.

Telephone: 01494 483273.

How to get there: Take a turning to the north-east (City Road!), signposted 'Radnage' and 'Bledlow Ridge', ½ mile east of Stokenchurch on the A40 and continue on the lane, ignoring all side turnings, until Bennett End Road is reached – a narrow lane. Follow this for about ½ mile to a small triangle of grass and a right-hand turn into Horseshoe Lane, another narrow one. The Three Horseshoes lies on the right, a few yards up the lane.

Parking: There is usually ample parking space in the large car park.

Length of the walk: 3 miles. Map: OS Pathfinder 1137 Watlington and Stokenchurch (inn GR 783973).

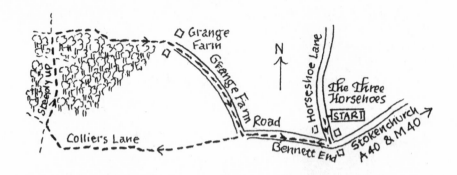

This magnificent countryside is beautiful at all times of the year – in the spring the woods are filled with bluebells, in summer skylarks sing above the cornfields, autumn-coloured woodland is truly spectacular and even a layer of crisp white snow can add to the area's special quality. This walk is mainly on bridleways so it can be muddy after wet weather.

The Walk

Turn left out of the pub and walk back the 20 yards or so, past a charming flint cottage, to the grass triangle with the lovely timber-framed Bennett End farmhouse on the opposite corner. Here turn right into Grange Farm Road to follow it between wood-fringed fields for a good ¼ mile. When the road bears sharply right, keep straight ahead onto the bridleway, Colliers Lane, and follow it straight ahead down this lovely valley, ignoring all side turnings, for about ¾ mile, with magnificent views all round and the post office tower outside Stokenchurch high on the wooded horizon ahead.

At a well-defined cross-track turn right to follow the path along the side of the wood then, bearing a little right again, follow the path on steeply uphill through the trees. Notice, as you walk, the bald places in the woodland left by the hurricane-shattered trees in the early 1990s and notice, too, how the great chalky plates of the upturned root systems are already well grown with vigorous rowan saplings and weeds to provide a habitat for small mammals and insects, they, in their turn, providing food for hungry owls and hawks and smaller birds of prey. Pause, on your way up, to turn round and drink in the marvellous landscape of wooded hills, ploughed or cultivated fields and the hugely wide expanse of the

The pleasant outlook from the pub's garden.

sky overhead. The setting is wonderfully peaceful, the only signs of humanity the small huddle of cottages among the trees below.

At the hilltop, ignore the cross-path and continue ahead across the wood and gently downhill to its edge, where you turn right onto a broad bridletrack and follow it through the tall, greeny-grey trunks of the beech trees along the wood edge to emerge onto a metalled lane, Grange Farm Road, again. Follow the road back, past the farm, turning sharply left onto the original stretch back to Horseshoe Lane on the left and the Three Horseshoes up on the right.

16 Coleshill
The Magpies

The scenery either side of the main road between Amersham and Beaconsfield is strikingly beautiful – rolling uplands and downlands of rich farmland interspersed with great wooded hills sweeping down into the valleys. It remains unspoiled, with no building but the pub and one farm from the hilltop watertower above Amersham to the outskirts of Beaconsfield.

The Magpies was an unpretentious Victorian alehouse, built in 1826 of red brick and tiles, with little ornamentation. Now it has been totally refurbished by the brewery company so that it is old-fashioned in its furnishing but completely modern in its service and general atmosphere. Its exterior is still that of the Victorian village pub but, alongside it and squarely onto the road, there is an enormous car park and, behind it, a huge, lawned garden bursting with children's playthings in all colours and sizes and including a bouncy castle. This is indeed a family pub! Beyond the playground is a patio-type area full of sturdy tables and benches and you enter the large bar through french windows. One side is set aside for dining and there are tables and banquettes all around the room. The U-shaped bar and busy food servery are staffed by a number of smiling and helpful young people.

You will find three real ales on handpump in this popular inn – Flowers Original, Boddingtons Bitter and Marston's Pedigree. Also on handpump are Murphy's stout and Strongbow cider. There is an impressive selection of wines by the glass and a good, comprehensive wine list. The traditional pub fare includes salad platters, ploughman's lunches, sandwiches and large filled baps. Among the main courses are fish and vegetarian dishes and there is a special menu for children. Food is served daily from 11.30 am to 10 pm. Opening hours for the bar are from 11 am to 11 pm on Monday to Saturday and from noon to 10.30 pm on Sunday.

Telephone: 01494 726754.

How to get there: The Magpies is at the junction of the A355 Amersham to Beaconsfield road with Magpie Lane, which leads to Coleshill village. It is about 2½ miles from Beaconsfield and 3 miles from Amersham.

Parking: A huge car park lies alongside the pub.

Length of the walk: 2 miles. Map: OS Pathfinder 1138 High Wycombe and Amersham (inn GR 955941).

This short walk is ideal for a hot summer's day leading, as it does, mostly through cool woodland dappled by sunlight and with some magnificent specimens of silver birch and huge beeches to delight the eye. The unspoilt scenery is wonderful at any time of year, but be prepared for muddy bridleways in the winter months.

The Walk
Turn left out of the pub to cross the end of Magpie Lane and then go over the main road, with care, to a footpath into woodland opposite. Follow the path uphill into the trees where, shortly, there is a deep and ancient chalk pit on the left. Keep to the main path, ignoring all side turnings and bearing slightly left and then right with it. Turn left at a major T-junction and follow this path to a lane, Bottrell Lane, where you turn right.

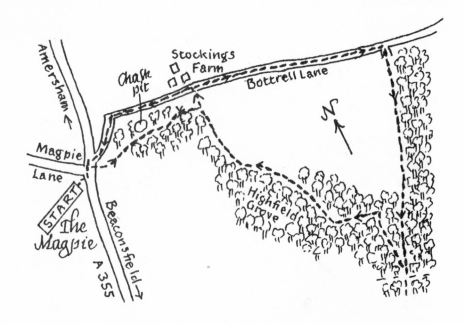

Walk up the lane between high, thick hedges of hazel and hawthorn with blackberries in huge clusters in the autumn and always tantalising glimpses of the lovely countryside through scarce gaps in the hedge. Walk past the farm buildings of Stockings Farm and the delightful 17th-century square red-brick Stockings House, set back in a lovely garden. Follow the lane round a gentle bend to a marked footpath on the right leading back into woodland, Highfield Grove, a charming mix of trees, some tall and elegant, some gnarled and squat.

Follow the well-defined footpath, ignoring all side turnings and past a junkyard on the right, for about ⅓ mile. Just after another deep chalk pit on the left, you will come to a major T-junction onto a wide bridleway, where you turn right. Follow the broad track ahead and then bear left close to the wood edge. After about 20 yards, turn right to follow the path along the edge of the wood again until Bottrell Lane is reached once more.

Now turn left to walk gently downhill on the lane through the beechwoods, passing a Forestry Commission picnic area at the woodside, and on to a layby off the A355. Turn left to walk along the layby and cross the busy road, with care, to reach the Magpies again.

17 Cadmore End
The Blue Flag

Cadmore End, part of the parish of Fingest, is a long-drawn-out little hamlet on the road between Stokenchurch and Marlow, which follows a high chalk ridge. It consists of a number of small red-brick houses peering out from dense copses of beech and mixed woodland and deep, often wooded, valleys on each side. Lying as it does close to the A40 and nearer still to the M40, there is a perpetual gentle drone of passing traffic, but this does little to mar the peaceful air of the community, which boasts a well-used church, a school and two pubs, the Ship at one end and the Blue Flag at the other.

The Blue Flag faces the road, its frontage a mere yard or two from it, a squat, two-storey, red-brick building, some 300 years old. It was once a coaching inn providing for travellers en route from London to Oxford – and it still performs that function. Beside the old inn has been built a 16-bedroomed, spacious, American-style hotel, backing onto woodland with extensive views over the countryside. Despite this, the genuine 'pub' atmosphere of the inn remains intact and there is an instant feeling of warmth and welcome as one enters. The large, L-shaped bar is staffed by a number of cheerful young people who ensure that no one has to wait long to be served. It is heavily beamed, with the usual decoration of brass ornaments, and it also has some fascinating photographs of early MGs on its walls. The floor is carpeted and set with tables, small and large, with padded settles and stools in a pleasantly muted shade of fabric. Beyond the bar is a delightfully furnished restaurant, light and airy. The cuisine is English/French, but especially interesting is the fact that the inn has its own smoking apparatus for preparing salmon and trout, the fish carefully chosen and purchased for their flavour, and so popular has this become that smoked fish is sold by the pound over the counter around Christmas and other festal times.

Fish, therefore, features large on the menu, which appears on a board in the bar and is extensive, unusual and interesting. Duck pâté (home-made, as is all the food) with hot toast, steaks, chicken, vegetarian dishes and ham and eggs vie with avocado and shrimp salad and crab in garlic butter. Another board lists mouthwatering sweets and a good selection of cheeses. There is also an excellent à la carte menu in the restaurant, where children may eat, although not permitted in the bar. Three house wines, one red and two white, are sold by the glass and there is a selective wine list. You will find four real ales – Wadworth 6X, Rebellion Mutiny from Marlow, London Pride and Morland Original. Opening times are from 10.30 am to 2.30 pm and 6 pm to 11 pm on weekdays, with the usual Sunday hours. Bar food is served from noon to 2 pm and 6.30 pm to 10 pm (9.15 pm on Sunday).

Telephone: 01494 881183.

How to get there: Cadmore End lies directly on the B482, west of High Wycombe. The Blue Flag is on the north side of the road, some 3 miles from the A40 at Stokenchurch. From this direction it comes upon one quite suddenly round a bend in the road, soon after the 'Cadmore End' sign.

Parking: There is a very large car park alongside the inn, in front of the hotel.

Length of the walk: 2½ miles. Map: OS Pathfinder 1137 Watlington and Stokenchurch (inn GR 778937).

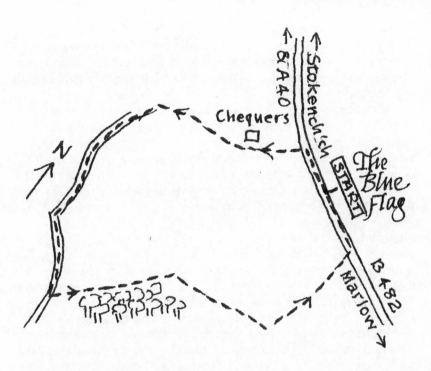

This short, gentle walk encapsulates the essence of the lovely sweeping Chiltern hillsides with their wood-fringed fields. The views are long and stupendous.

The Walk
Turn right out of the pub and walk up the road for 20 yards. Cross with care by a pretty flint house to a marked footpath on the left. Go over two stiles to follow a path across a small field and over a fence under a tree opposite. Continue across the field to another two stiles in the hedge on the other side. Go over the stiles to walk along the headland of the field, then downhill on its right-hand side, with the hedge and a sheep fence on the right. Tucked up in the far right-hand corner is a stile, which you cross onto a steeply stepped bank leading on to a lane beside the gazebo of the splendid garden of Chequers House.

Turn left to follow the lane downhill, ignoring side turnings, to reach a well-marked and defined footpath on the left leading into Hanger Wood. Follow the path fairly steeply uphill through the mixed woodland, emerging into open country at the top. Pause here to take in the spectacular view of the whole of the Turville Valley opened out below and the misty blue hills two or three miles beyond it. Ibstone House is the large white edifice a little to the north-west and the village of Fingest straggles along the lane toward the church.

Follow the path into the open field and turn left at the next hedge to follow a marked path, keeping on the right first the tall, thick hedge and then a handsome house set in a lawned and shrubby garden. The path emerges onto the road some 150 yards from the Blue Flag. Turn left and cross over to return to it. There is always a certain amount of traffic, so it is advisable to walk with care, keeping to the grass verge along the roadside.

Places of interest nearby
Just down the road from Cadmore End, at Booker Airfield, is *The Blue Max Collection*. This is a unique museum of flying aeroplanes that have starred in such films as 'Those Magnificent Men in their Flying Machines' and 'Indiana Jones'. The exhibits are still being used for film and television work today. The museum also has a restoration programme for recovered aircraft and they are currently working on two D-Day Spitfires and other classic aircraft. There is a souvenir shop and restaurant facilities elsewhere on the airfield. The collection is open daily from 10 am to 5 pm between March and November. The Blue Max museum is at Wycombe Air Park, Clay Hill, Booker, Marlow. Telephone 01494 529432 or 449810.

18 Turville
The Bull and Butcher

The centre of this charming village, situated in a deep, dry Chiltern valley, is a minute triangular village green. Cottages, half-timbered, thatched, flint and tile, cluster around it. To the west is St Mary's church, of scrubbed flint exterior and entered by a simple 13th-century south door. Stained glass includes pieces with armorial bearings of the 16th, 17th and 18th centuries. A lunette in the nave has a delicate white hand and lily, executed by John Piper to commemorate the beatification of the church. The whole village is overlooked benignly by the large smock mill on the hill above, with its white timber upper stage and sails and a great black cap set dramatically on the skyline.

The Bull and Butcher has been an alehouse since the early 17th century. It is rambling and whitewashed, with a tall white brick chimney and low-ceilinged interior. There is a huge, much-needed parking area beside the pub and a long, lawned garden with plenty of practical tables and chairs – delightfully colourful and sunny on warm summer days, although a tree near the road affords shade.

The smock mill, situated above the village of Turville.

Inside there are small, cosy bars to left and right and a little dining area tucked up in a sunny corner. The whole is carpeted and sensibly furnished with wooden tables and chairs. Horse brasses and implements decorate the deep inglenook fireplaces and there is a dark wood dresser full of quaint brass ornaments.

This is a Brakspear house so the draught ales are the excellent Old Ale, Bitter and Special. Lager is also on draught. House wines, red and white, are available by the glass and there is a small but well-chosen selection of wines for sale by the bottle. All around are blackboards proclaiming the day's menus, with items ranging from rump steaks, through curries and chicken, to fish dishes (perhaps spicy baked cod), sole and salmon. There are plenty of salads from which to choose, ploughman's lunches and five sorts of pâté served with chunks of delicious brown crusty bread. The puddings are very tempting too. Meals are served at lunchtime and in the evening every day and the inn is open from noon to 3 pm and 5.30 pm to 11 pm (10.30 pm on Sunday). On some Saturdays and high days it is open all day. Children are welcome both in the little dining area and in the garden.

Telephone: 01491 638283.

How to get there: Turville is about 8 miles west of High Wycombe and 7 miles from junction 5 of the M40 motorway at Stokenchurch from where it can be approached through Ibstone along a very pretty, unclassified lane. For Turville turn right at the lane end, a T-junction, and the village is about ¾ mile further on.

Parking: You can park at the pub.

Length of the walk: 2½ miles. Map: OS Pathfinder 1137 Watlington and Stokenchurch (inn GR 768911).

This short walk encompasses some of the most beautiful and dramatic scenery to be found in the Chilterns. It traverses the valley floor and then there is a short, steep climb to breathtaking views of a patchwork of fields and woodland.

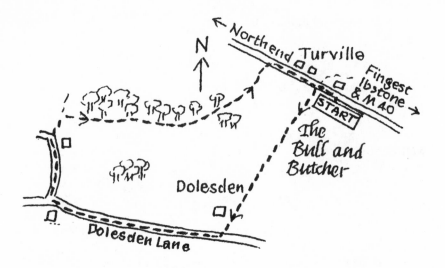

The Walk

Turn left out of the pub and left into a tiny lane behind the village green, which leads past some pretty old cottages to the now, sadly, disused village school. The lane continues ahead into a waymarked footpath between high, overhanging hedges and then bursts out into the open across a large field with wide views all round. Walk straight across the field to Dolesden Farm, a very charming red-brick house set in a pretty garden with a duck pond in one corner.

Turn right at the farm into Dolesden Lane and walk up it, gently uphill by fields, bordered on the right by a long tongue of mixed woodland above a wide field where pheasants stand, listening and gleaning, and rabbits run into their burrows on the wood edge.

At a path (signposted on both sides of the lane) turn right to mount a rather awkward stile set in the bank and walk ahead, steeply uphill, keeping the small brake of trees on the right. This is the only steep climb on the walk and it doesn't last long. At the top of the field turn right onto the drive of Turville Court, a small 17th to 18th-century house set in a very beautiful garden, with spectacular views all round. Almost immediately, take the waymarked path on the left into woodland – Churchfield Wood. After about 75 yards, turn right onto a path running alongside the wood edge. Springtime is wonderful here, when the ground is carpeted with the brilliant blue of massed bluebells, the air filled with their scent, sweet and heady, and, above, the cool, cathedral-like vault of pale green beech

Turville village.

leaves tops the tall, straight tree trunks. Here, too, pheasants scuttle and rattle through the dried leaves of autumn and rise, screeching noisily, at one's approach.

The path meanders gently downhill with marvellous wide views over the valley and away to the white mill on the hill ahead. Where the path forks, keep to the right along the wood edge. Bear sharply left at another fork to follow white arrows downhill and cross a bridleway at the foot of the hill. Go over the stile here and turn right again, continuing on the path to the lane. Turn right to return to the pub, passing the encampment of some local bodgers just off the road.

⑲ Wooburn Common
The Royal Standard

Wooburn Common itself is an area of pretty, mixed woodland bisected by numerous narrow lanes and paths and edged with prosperous farms and small cottages.

The Royal Standard is a low-beamed, 18th-century pub with a multitude of small windows, overhung by eaves and peering out onto the road. It is of red brick and tile and its roof curves every which way! The frontage is a courtyard with tables and benches and flower tubs and, within, there is a welcoming atmosphere in the long, carpeted bar, which has a neat dining area to the left and a games room to the right. Down three steps is a charming snug with dining facilities, all nicely furnished with heavy wood tables and assorted stools, chairs and banquettes padded in a muted pink fabric. Around the walls are prints of glamorously clad cavalrymen of various regiments.

Cask ales, Brakspear Special and Greene King IPA, are alongside those on handpump, Boddingtons, Flowers Original, Whitbread and Marston's Pedigree, and there is a regularly changing guest.

Beside these, you will find two lagers, Murphy's stout, Guinness and Strongbow cider, so the choice is wide. A long list of wines, many of which can be sold by the glass, is also available. Three boards in the bar display the large range of very reasonably priced food, from starters of jacket skins and cheese, through main courses of steaks, gammon, lamb and chicken dishes and a vegetarian Kiev, to a staggering variety of sweets. For those wanting a light lunch, there is a good menu of snacks, including huge sandwiches of granary bread, ploughman's of cheese or ham with salad, jacket potatoes with appropriate fillings and jumbo sausage and chips. A big bowl of delicious home-made celery and Stilton soup accompanied by a 'doorstep' crammed with chicken and lettuce and a side salad was excellent value on a recent visit. Children are welcome in the eating area and in the gravelly garden outside. Opening times are from 11 am to 11 pm on weekdays and from noon on a Sunday. Telephone: 01628 521121.

How to get there: Wooburn and Wooburn Common lie south of Beaconsfield. From the A40 at the west end of the town, take the road signposted for Wooburn Common, Burnham and Taplow.

Odds Farm Park.

Continue for about 1½ miles, bearing left at a Y-junction and turning left, again as for Wooburn Common, shortly afterwards. The Royal Standard lies on the left 100 yards up the road.

Parking: There is a largish car park alongside the pub.

Length of the walk: 3 miles. Map: OS Pathfinder 1157 Maidenhead and Marlow (inn GR 923876).

The high ridge on which this walk is taken is one between two deep river valleys – the Wye at High Wycombe and the Thames at Taplow. The walk is level, there are few stiles and the views extend over wide expanses of peaceful farmland and broad bands of mixed woodland.

The Walk
Turn right out of the pub and walk a few yards along the road, then go right again into a lane between pleasant cottage gardens. Keep straight ahead past Castlemans Farm, with the children's fun-farm, Odds Farm Park, on the right. After about ½ mile take the signed footpath on the left beside a large holly bush. Follow the

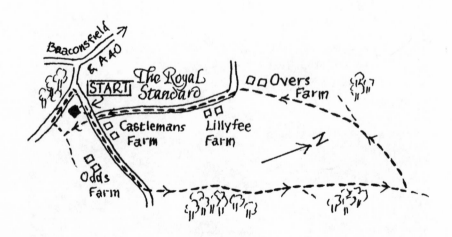

path over the stile and alongside the field, with lovely wide views of the rich farmland around. Continue along the wood edge and on, over a stile, into the woodland, turning right to walk again alongside the edge of the trees on the far side. Follow the well-defined path on, past a plantation of new trees and a track signposted 'Hall Barn', to a large gap in the hedge ahead.

Go through the gap and turn immediately left to walk alongside the hedge on the left and huge earthworks on the right. Soon you will come to a gap in the hedge, waymarked. Turn left to go through it and then immediately right to follow the path to the opposite hedge, where you go left and take the narrow path round the field edge, with a wire-fenced quarry on the right and a straggly old hedge on the left, followed by a wire fence.

At the end of the wire fence, at a gap close to the next hedge, turn left to follow a path across a bit of field and then between tall hedges to Overs Farm. Turn left at the junction of the farm road with the lane and walk down it, past Lillyfee Farm, to Castlemans Farm again. At the T-junction there, cross the road to a marked footpath in the opposite hedge. Follow the path through a gate alongside part of Odds Farm Park and, on reaching the car park, turn right to walk down through it to the main road again. Turn right to walk the few yards back to the car park of the Royal Standard.

Places of interest nearby
Odds Farm Park is a delight for children of all ages. There are the usual opportunities for the young ones to feed lambs and chickens and to pet some of the other small animals such as rabbits and guinea pigs. There are 'under cover' play areas and other facilities including a tea room, gift shop and a 'new mother and baby' room. The farm park is open daily from April to September between 10 am and 5 pm and Thursday to Sunday from October to March between 10 am and 4 pm (daily during half-term holidays). There are special rates for groups and further information is available on 01628 520188.

The Dog and Badger

The Dog and Badger stands squarely on the road at a crossroads and is backed by a very steeply sloping and wooded hill so that it almost seems to have been carved from the hillside, as was its huge car park alongside. The 16th-century whitewashed and timbered inn was once a rendezvous for Nell Gwynn and some of her many admirers and, later, members of the notorious Hell-Fire Club, founded by Sir Francis Dashwood, came to drink at its ample bar from the club's home at Medmenham Abbey. Until 1899 banns of marriage were read by the Parish Clerk in the inn before they were published in the church opposite.

Because of its situation there is only room outside for a small patio garden behind the inn. Vines, bearing grapes in season, grow over the elegant pergola and afford shade on hot days. The bar occupies the whole ground floor of the pub, with a little snug just inside the door from the car park. Dining tables are set at the far end of the bar. The room is simply and pleasantly furnished and there is a separate restaurant where children are welcome.

There are five real ales on draught – Ruddles, Wethered Bitter, Flowers Original, Brakspear Special and Wadworth 6X. Five house wines are sold by the glass and there is also a good wine list. An interesting selection of specials is displayed on a blackboard in the bar. As well as an excellent menu of hot and cold main courses, including fish and chicken dishes, there is a wide range of sandwiches with a choice of white or brown bread. Splendid value are filled baguettes (there's a delicious spicy sausage filling) and stotties, a huge bap with a variety of middles, including coronation chicken, both served with chips and salad garnish. Opening times are from 11.30 am to 3 pm and 6 pm to 11 pm on Monday to Saturday and from noon to 3 pm and 7 pm to 10.30 pm on Sunday.
Telephone: 01491 571362.

How to get there: The inn lies on the A4155 Marlow to Henley road, about 4 miles from Marlow and on the north side of the crossroads.

Parking: There is ample parking space alongside the inn.

Length of the walk: 3¼ miles. Maps: OS Pathfinder 1156 Henley and Wallingford and 1157 Maidenhead and Marlow (inn GR 806845).

The walk leads through the village of Medmenham, the only remaining truly Thames-side village in Buckinghamshire, and along a peaceful stretch of the river to return over the fields by ancient footpaths.

The Walk
Cross the road from the pub and turn left to the crossroads, where you turn right to walk down the lane into Medmenham, past the church and a pleasant variety of houses and cottages, some of old flint and brick, some timber-framed and some more modern. On the far side of a small white bridge over Abbotsbrook there is evidence on the left of the existence of the abbey which was taken over by Sir Francis Dashwood when it had fallen into disuse. The Hell-Fire Club was founded here in the mid-18th century.
On reaching the river at the now defunct ferry point, turn right to walk along the broad towpath. Here the river is fairly wide and

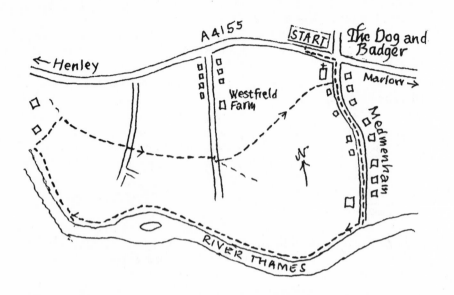

fast flowing through strips of meadows backed by low-lying, tree-topped hills on both sides, while ahead lie the higher, grander, heavily-wooded hills which rise between Maidenhead and Wargrave and are locally known as 'the paps of Maidenhead'. Soon the impressive edifice of Culham Court appears high on the left bank.

Carry on along the riverside path for about 1¼ miles and turn right at a whitewashed thatched cottage to walk alongside the field, away from the river. At the top of the field, ignore both stile and gate and turn right to follow a path, keeping the wire fence on the left. At the end of this field is a small gate but its far side is barred by three strands of threatening-looking barbed wire, so turn slightly right to emerge, in a few yards, onto a concrete farm track. Turn right and then, very shortly, left to follow another concrete track as it weaves round a field of contentedly grazing cattle. Close to the end of the path, on the far side of the field, is a stile on the right. Go over the stile and walk across the field ahead, bearing slightly left to a gate in the tall hedge opposite. Through the gate, walk leftward around the next field, keeping the trees close on the left. Climb over the stile at the field end onto a lane, which you cross to a stile opposite into another field.

Follow the path straight across this field to a stile in the left-hand corner leading into a small brake of woodland. Follow the narrow

94

path through the wood and out past a high brick wall on the right and the church on the left to the lane through Medmenham village, where you turn left to return to the crossroads and the Dog and Badger.

Places of interest nearby

If you would like to know more about the notorious Hell-Fire Club and the dashing Sir Francis, why not visit *West Wycombe Caves* at West Wycombe Park? Here, you can explore the caves under West Wycombe hill and see life-sized models of the 2nd baronet and some of his cronies. The caves are open daily from March to October between 11 am and 5.30 pm but opening is restricted to weekends and bank holidays from November to February. Telephone 01494 533739 for further details. The house and gardens of *West Wycombe Park* are administered by the National Trust and are open to the public. Sir Francis Dashwood had the grounds and house substantially re-modelled in the mid 18th century and the result is, as one would expect from the founder of the Dilettanti Society, rather intricate and certainly theatrical. Telephone 01494 524411 for further details.